From the Library of
Leon Salzman

LOGIC AND EXISTENCE

LOGIC and EXISTENCE

MARTIN FOSS

PHILOSOPHICAL LIBRARY
New York, N. Y.

© Copyright, 1962,
by Philosophical Library, Inc.
15 East 40th Street, New York

All rights reserved
Library of Congress Catalogue Card No. 61-18687
Printed in the United States of America

CONTENTS

Introduction   vii

FIRST PART: ABSTRACTION

I.	Fact and Order	3
II.	Function and Infinity	18
III.	Extension, Substance, and Causality	27
IV.	Concept, Law and Purpose	41

SECOND PART, REALITY

V.	Life, World and Existence	63
VI.	Destiny and Freedom	111
VII.	Sin, Guilt, Sacrifice and Love	147
VIII.	Value and Creation	176
	Conclusion	216
	Notes	222
	Index	237

INTRODUCTION

The philosopher's problem is where to begin. Archimedes the scientist could claim: Give me a foothold, a place where I am firmly rooted, and I shall move the world. This is, indeed, what science does and is allowed to do: to conceive the world according to a certain perspective, any perspective which makes for a consistent view. This, however, is just what the philosopher cannot do. He has no use for a world seen from a certain angle, and he would prefer to extinguish himself and all perspectives in order to reach his goal.

Injustice has been done to the philosopher by those who call him "subjective." He is and always has been in love with objectivity. The problem of the "subject" became important only as the danger and pitfall to his objectivity. To transcend the subject has been the effort of every great philosophy, and this is even so with the youngest movement of Western thought, Existentialism, although not all its representatives seem to understand its core.

The history of philosophy can be regarded as a constant crusade against the relativity of psychological perspectives. Plato had to rise against the Sophists, Leibniz and Kant against the Empiricists. From the very dawn of philosophical inquiry this crusade combatted not only subjective thinking, but even all forms of particularity, and its combat was heated by religious fervor. The crusade assumed however, very different patterns in the East and in the West. In Asia every subjective particularity was drowned in "Nothingness," a reality of a very special character, reached in an emotional intensification, a concentration of will. The "Naught of Nirvana," as we find it in India, is absolute and all-comprehensive, and it is dynamic, because it is the result of a total concentration of will. And that which the will had to conquer and to extinguish is the realm of distinction, of analysis, or, simply, of thought. It is in fact the "Naught of thought," the absolute negation of the sphere of thought. Negation as absolute, not as a merely relative negation, is directed against a total realm of apparent reality and extinguishes this realm by means of a superior power. The superior power is emotion, working against the intellect. But the paradox is that emotion itself, although the instrument by which the subject freed itself from the multitude of distinctions is a powerful link to subjectivity: it becomes a danger and has also to be suppressed in an ultimate effort to reach objectivity. In spite of the fact that the road to Nirvana was paved by emotional intensification, emotion has now to be abandoned too. This is the fundamental paradox of Eastern philosophy: Emotion is both a means of lifting beyond appearance, and incurably tied to appearance—a wing and a weight.

The West has traveled a very different road, trying to conquer the particular. Here it was the sober and unemotional discovery of the "universal," the abstract "Being as such" which was destined to overcome particular subjectivity. Not "Nothing" as an emotional conquest and concentration, but "Being" as an abstract expansion of thought stands out as the expression of Western objectivity. Metaphysics means for the West the realm of Being, just as it means for the East the realm of "Naught." But in order to reach this height of abstract Being the West had to plunge into a paradox similar to that of the East: The instrument by which the West transcends the particular is thought, analyzing and synthesizing thought. But the Being which is intended in the process of analysis, differentiation and synthesis, is itself undifferentiated and not put together in a synthesis, transcendent to every and any distinction, and it is therefore foreign to the distinguishing activity which worked up toward it. Just as emotion had ministered to the Naught in order only to be itself emotionally suppressed, so discursive reasoning has disclosed abstract Being in order only to be shut out and replaced by the enigmatic and mysterious "intuition" which no thinking can explain and which seems a foreign element in Western thought.

East and West have gone opposite roads. The East can not understand the sublimity of Western "Being." If the East wants to give a positive meaning to its ultimate reality, it may call it "Life" or "Soul," and this is indeed how "Brahma" is most appropriately conceived. And Life and Soul recall the emotional origin of this transcendence of particularity. The West, on the other hand, has no real understanding of the Nirvana or Naught and attacks absolute "Nothingness," wherever it finds it, as nonsensical, as unthinkable. In this attack even the most extreme poles of Western thought, Plato and Bergson, unite. For, indeed, as a concept, as an abstract thought, the absolute naught is meaningless. Thus has this road been blocked for the West; and only negative theology has in Western thought, perhaps under Eastern influence, got an inkling of the ineffable, yet experienced, naught of holiness and absolute Reality.

Although their roads are thus very different, East and West do meet in their aspiration to transcend subjectivity. But the fact that each in its way has to cope with a fundamental paradox shows that their approaches are not the truth, at least not the whole truth. Paradoxes are a symptom of onesidedness and distortion. The full truth must lie in the union of their approaches. In the course of this work such a union will be attempted.

LOGIC AND EXISTENCE

FIRST PART: ABSTRACTION

I. FACT AND ORDER

Philosophical analysis can proceed in two different directions, depending on its point of departure. It may start in the fullness of reality, in the abundance of an intensive experience, in God, in World, in Existence,—inexhaustible and infinitely rich—, and pass from here, step by step, into the last elements which constitute this experience. In doing this it will end in the poorest and simplest product of abstraction, scarcely experienced. This is one way open to the philosopher. The other way starts with the very last element, in which the first way ended, and it ascends from here into the fullness of a complex reality.

The first of these two approaches is very tempting: for here the seeker is supported by his immediate experience, near to him and familiar, so that he is carried along by what he feels is true. He is able to measure every one of his steps by the standard of a living experience and can correct any deviation from the truth by what is already at his disposal and lends itself to him without effort: his very life and the treasure of its accumulated wisdom. The disadvantage of this procedure is, however, that the progress of the philosopher implies continual loss, that the atmosphere around him becomes thinner at every step, and that he finds himself at the end so far from reality and experience that contact with them breaks, so that he may condemn his whole adventure as disappointing and fruitless. On the other hand, the start in pure abstraction asks for a "tour de force," a leap into that which is farthest from experience, unfamiliar, unconvincing, and the seeker, supported by nothing but his urge for an unknown truth, may lose heart and bog down in a desert of bloodless constructions. Hard though this may be, the reward is sublime: From moment to moment the poverty of his arid beginning gives way to a growing richness; the world around him will alight and blossom, until at last the fullness of truth, the abundance of reality sheds its radiance on the dark phases of a previous development.

We have chosen this latter way and now face the hardship of its initial stages, the thorny road and the violent breaking away from all that is familiar. But this, indeed, is the road which Western thought traditionally traveled, and it has actually made Western philosophy a "tour de force," highly suspect to the many who desire to be carried by immediate experience. There is an ascetic flavor, a tragic aridity in Western thought for which the attitude of a Parmenides is most respresentative. It was Parmenides who denied himself the support which the familiar variety of things provides, and who chose instead the sublime but arid "Being" of pure abstraction.

But what is abstraction, and by what right is it separated from reality, as if it were set over and against it? Is this absraction a non-reality, a non-being? Has it fallen away from reality, as Lucifer fell away from God? Such a breaking away from reality would indeed be a fall, an original sin in the realm of philosophy, and the thinker who committed it would be damned to the loss of reality forever. For no path can lead from an abstraction divorced from reality back to its fullness. Thought would circle around itself and would usurp the role of God before creation.

There is, however, no way of denying it: At the start of Metaphysics an abyss opens between thought and being, and man, the thinker, stands at its precipice, gazing longingly at the opposite shore. It is this longing to bridge the gap and heal the breach which poses the first, the fundamental problem of Metaphysics. No wonder that the solution which immediately presented itself as a premature solution, is to turn away from reality and to reside totally in subjective thought. The primitive and the child cannot face the reality which rises beyond thought, they avoid the encounter with "facts" by letting the facts be absorbed by their thought, by an abstraction which, divorced from any objective experience, is pure invention. This transformation of facts by invention is what we call "phantasy" or, with the color of indignation, a "lie." These people lie and imagine, and a great part of what we call "play" is an imaginative transformation of the factual, giving delight to the immature mind. It is not so much "imitation" that the child and the primitive enjoy, for imitation is based on respect for facts and a withdrawal from one's own subjectivity: It is rather exaggeration, transformation which is the attitude of the immature, as phantastic as possible, caricaturing and inventing instead of observing, subjecting instead of freeing, disguising instead of revealing. The incredible has always had its attraction for the undeveloped man and for the masses.

In this play of phantasy reality disappears: it becomes a dream at the mercy of an unfettered abstraction. Phantasy may dream of an independent reality and may even worship this, its own creature and puppet, as if it were its destiny. But, in fact, it is only its own fear or vanity, its own lust or terror which feigns a reality worthy of devotion.

Reality is here definitely lost, absorbed in a triumphant but anarchic subjectivity. Such subjectivity will lend itself to psychological analysis and will interest from this point of view, but it has no philosophical status. Philosophy submits to psychological findings, wherever reality has been lost and only a subjective play of mental functions is left. But as such a subjective attitude is the starting ground of primitive man, remainders of it will be found even on higher levels, and it will be especially the terminology used which will outlive the meaning and will show psychological atavisms in metaphysical statements. Even a Plato used the term "idea," taken from a subjective psychological level, in order to convey a reality beyond any subjective ideation.

Philosophy begins beyond this psychological level, and, to put it still more strongly: Philosophy will start in breaking away from subjectivity, openly and uncompromisingly sacrificing the subjectivity of thought for the sake of an independent, objective, and absolute reality. Instead of drowning the fact in a subjective thought-process, a humble and devoted thought will subject itself, cancel itself in the face of fact, "abstracting" from itself and from its own interference, and thus become an instrument for approaching a fact which is indeed independent and truly absolute.

No wonder that such an ascetic attitude presupposes a certain maturity of the race and of the individual, and that Metaphysics does not start before the dawn of civilization. Self-denial is at the bottom of the metaphysical concern; it is a moral attitude, and so morality and philosophy are linked together in the youth of metaphysical inquiry. Not only the East was strongly aware of this: Plato also regarded the True and the Good as one and the same. But this self-denying attitude, in spite of being an act of willing, is bare of any subjective enjoyment, of any awareness of or reflection upon its own activity. Thought, cancelling itself in the face of fact, subjecting itself to fact, receives in its turn an objective and even absolute character. The objectivity of this thought-process, absolute, independent and constitutive, has led thinkers to raise it to Divine status, as a thought which thinks itself. But it is far more complex and paradoxical: The life-process of Brahma may turn into itself, and the Aristotelian "thought which thinks itself," has been interpreted in a way resembling Eastern Divinity. But the fundamental metaphysical thought is a thought which, far from thinking itself, "abstracts" from itself, as the prototype of all abstraction, negating itself; and in doing this it becomes instrumental to the independent and absolute fact from which it receives objectivity and absoluteness in its turn. This may seem paradoxical, but it is indeed the experience of any discoverer whose thinking, totally subjected to the discovered fact, loses the last shadow of arbitrary subjectivity.

Fact as independent and objective is, however, so utterly isolated that it is just fact and nothing more. As sublime as the self-effacement of thought is—and this sublime forgetting of one's own subjectivity will always be the attitude of devotion to something greater than oneself—the fact which is constituted by this effacement of thought is opaque, closed to understanding. Thought withdrawn from fact can only grasp the "thatness" of the fact and nothing more. It is a naked, a brutal fact that results from this withdrawal; it has no qualities. Thinking has silenced itself in the presence of this fact. Thought can state only that fact is "absolute," that it is not derived from anything and does not lead to anything. It is what we may call an "accident." It falls upon us and has to be taken for what it is.

Thus our road starts in the darkness of the accidental. This is a hard start for intelligent man. It has always been man's endeavour to dissolve the accidental by the light of his intelligence. But this is exactly what can not be done at this point. "Accident" does not mean here subjective ignorance, it is a "necessary accident," necessary in the sense of absence of dependence and connection, of any tie whatsoever. This is the literal meaning of "absolute." The absolute may at times comfort us in its stable detachment as a haven of necessity; it may however at times frighten in its unpredictable accidentality, and so Mythology has personified both aspects, now as the inscrutable Tyche, now as the stable and reliable Dike.

Fact is closed to thought, but belongs to thought which, however, does not so much "think" the fact as limit itself in the face of fact.[1] It is from this absoluteness of fact that thought in its humility and self-effacement receives absoluteness in its turn, the absoluteness of a process which negates itself and is as an absolute "nought" over and against the being of fact. The dominant role, however, which fact played, as the meaning of all thinking, was so strong in Western culture which worshipped fact and built its edifice of science on fact that the negating process, the nought, scarcely could hold its place besides the all-powerful Being; and although the dynamic but unstable process of a negating thought was recognized as the ground out of which fact rises in its unquestionable absoluteness and necessity,[2] the status of Not-being and its role besides Being was one of the most intricate mysteries in Western philosophy. In a naive but audacious way mythology coped with this problem and took the edge off it by clothing the harsh and clashing abstractions in material attire. The Orphic cosmology makes Night the cradle of a factual being, an empty and dark entity is here responsible for a thing which emerges out of its emptiness.[3] This materialization of the fundamental duality of Non-Being and Being finds an even clearer expression in early Science, where it serves as the most powerful device of systematization. Non-Being appears here as the "Vacuum" which represents the negating and at the same time constitutive process of thought, while the fact of Being is understood as the "atom" for which the vacuum is responsible in its isolation and absoluteness. The atom is indeed the closed, opaque fact, absolute, necessary but at the same time accidental, unrelated, without distinction or structure, and thus unanalyzable, indivisible, that is "atomos." The Vacuum as its counterpart is equally necessary and opaque, the "nought" which, in spite of being a nought, is an entity in its own right, as Democritus already knew. Atom and vacuum, as materializations of fact and nought, have been put by Science into the sense-world, and so the scientist has never stopped looking for them among the things of perception. Scientists have claimed to observe atoms, but then again they acknowledged that atom and vacuum were rather products of invention, of mental construction, and thus merely subjective and expedient. But both of these interpretations are inadequate: Atom and Vacuum are metaphysical necessities, objective and absolute, neither merely observed nor merely invented, but forced upon the mind, revealing in material terms the metaphysical tension between fact and a negating process. Because of their fundamental character Science was able to interpret atom and vacuum in ever different ways, filling into these unobserved and uninvented frames whatever fitted the needs of the scientific situation of the time. The history of Science could well be written as the history of the ever changing character of atom and vacuum from the time of Democritus until now. The atom was first conceived as an infinitely small piece of matter; but then it became gradually deprived of its simple nature, was understood as a load of energy, as a center of forces, and even as a mere crossing-point of stresses in a field. The Vacuum in turn was interpreted by Plato as "χώρα," that is as a kind of empty space, not clearly definable, a "hybrid" concept; but then its negative status seemed to be better expressed as matter which deprived of form was instrumental for this very form, a glaring paradox, showing its dubious origin; and our modern Physics has been no less paradoxical in conceiving the vacuum as a "curved space" responsible for the course of facts in its orbit.

While Science found its own version to cope with the paradox of Being and Not-Being, metaphysics was exposed to a harder test, uncompromising and fully aware of the difficulties involved in the unification of Being with a self-negating thought, of fact and process. Tentatively and hesitatingly early thinkers simply placed both, Being and Not-being, side by side and thus were faced with a form of abstraction, difficult to elucidate, the "relation." The problems involved in "relation" are covered up and hidden through the use of this form of abstraction throughout the centuries, but it still remains a complex and questionable device; a unity which holds apart what it unites, a one which is a many, a combination of elements which are separated as well as brought together, and it was this separation, this mutual "exclusion," the exclusion of incomparable elements, fact and process, which gave rise to this fundamental but enigmatic form. The "relation of exclusion" is the cradle of all relation, early discovered and a source of wonder.[4]

Metaphysics can not stop at this solution, which can only be a provisional and preparatory solution, pointing to a more subtle unity. Certainly, the relation of exclusion, of "contradiction": "A excludes Non-A," became a guide to our thinking. But metaphysically it is deficient: it does not really unite, not really relate; it holds apart, separates, excludes and leaves the terms thus separated in utter vagueness. To know nothing but exclusion, conveys no meaning to the excluded. Furthermore: In "relating" fact and process and attempting to bring these incomparable entities into one unity, not only the absoluteness of both, but also their specific character is destroyed, they are assimilated to each other in spite of the "exclusion," [5] and thus a tighter and more stable unity is prepared, a unity in which these terms, having lost absoluteness and factuality, serve the absoluteness and factuality of the unity as such: It is the "relation of Identity" which is born in this way, a relation which is itself absolute, has absorbed in its own form all factuality and has become a factual, absolute and all-comprehensive "structure," but a structure which besides being stable and factual is also the absolute necessity of process, is a "structure" as well as a "structuring." Into this absolute structure the terms feed as mere means of identification, weakened, deprived not only of factuality but of all character of their own, separated merely for the sake of vanishing in the oneness of the structure, identified and swallowed up in this absolute and all-embracing unity.[6]

It is in this way that the "Relation of Identity" grows out of the merely preparatory relation of exclusion, as the fulfillment of relational unity, but at the same time as the fulfillment of unity between fact and process, between Being and Thought. Thus this relation of Identity in its absoluteness and all-comprehensive character is the realization of the Parmenidean vision: Being and Thought is one. As such an all-comprehensive unity it became the ground of metaphysical systematization, the foundation of all philosophical abstraction. At times hypostatized to Divine status, it has, in the history of thought, assumed ever new forms: We find this identity of Being and thought, of fact and process, in Leibniz's monad as a structural principle as well as a dynamic entity; we find it in Kant's Transcendental Apperception as the ground of all lawful and objective stability, but also as an "activity of unification." And if we go back to ancient thought, we find the same identification of structure and process in the last and wisest dialogues of Plato who discovered a factual cosmic structure, τὸ δημιοῦργοῦν," clarified as a formal cause, an objective μετρον"; but who, not satisfied by this objective structure, supplemented it by an activity of the soul to which he gave the same name "ὁ δημιοῦργός," thus recognizing the identity of the structure and the structuring process.[7] The metaphysics of Aristotle follows the same line: his categories of nature are factual, but they are at the same time categories of thought and as such of a processual character.

Thus the relation of identity fulfills, as factual "structure" and processual "structuring," the Parmenidean vision of a unity between Being and Thought, fact and process, and this unity will be revealed on every stage of our investigation, until, as identity of essence and existence, it will disclose the reality of creation.[8] But at this early stage of our analysis the metaphysical unity will present itself as the more sober idea of an all-comprehensive "Order," an order which is also an "ordering." Order is that most comprehensive kind of "being" which is at the same time Thought, a structure and a structuring.[9] It is indeed "one" as Parmenides states, one and indivisible, but as a mediating thought it contains a plurality of terms which vanish, however, in their identification, so that negation and plurality are present but integrated into the unity.[10] That Order as a factual structure is also to be regarded as a thought-process, conveys to this included thought the absoluteness and objectivity without which thought would be a subjective imposition. It is this objectivity of thought, beyond a merely psychic procedure which allows the terms in the structure to be both: separated in exclusion and united in identity. Analysis separates them and synthesis unites the separated. And although analysis and synthesis are separate in time, when subjective psychic procedures, they are here, as contained in the objective structure, stabilized, united as the expression of the identified Order itself.

This structure of Order will be traced, however, and expounded in separate thought-processes which retain objectivity as the exposition of the identifying order-structure, even when developed in a subjective procedure. It is "Logic" which in this way expounds the processes of analysis and synthesis as clarifications of the order-structure in which they are contained and of which they expose the essential identity. Logic is restricted to the relation of that identity and that only. This restriction is the strength of Logic, its exactitude, objectivity and absoluteness; but it is also its weakness and responsible for the narrowness and poverty which is characteristic of Logic.[11] The objective order of identity which Logic traces underlies in its strength and exactitude the whole of nature and it is therefore fundamental for the system and method of Natural Science, as this was rightly stated.[12] But it should not be overlooked that Logic and the Order of identity, because of their narrowness and poverty, are unable to exhaust the content of Science which has to cope with variety and difference too; Science is just as much concerned with the specification of facts as with their absorption by an identical structure. This variety, difference, and specification of facts will have to be considered at a later stage of our work. It may at times confuse the pure and stable order of identity and Logic, so that the rules of Logic may clash with the experienced facts; and thus it may happen that a statement preserves its correctness from the logical point of view, but that, in spite of logical correctness, it may be meaningless or even non-sensical from the point of view of empirical facts and their differentiation. Such a clash of Logic with experience would indeed be impossible, if the terms in the order of identity, as pure order, were facts and had the weight and positive independence which facts have.

But here we are faced with the paradoxical character of the terms in the logical order. These terms are not facts, for the only true fact is the order itself in which these terms are absorbed and vanish. The terms "are" only for the sake of vanishing in the relational structure. They have no independence, they are not at all existent in their own right; they are merely stations of identity, they "signify" identity and that is all they do; they are nothing if not significations of order. As mere significations they are expressed by "signs." A sign is nothing in itself: it points only to something for which it is the sign. Therefore only signs do full justice to Logic. Signs, not facts, are separated as terms of order, and there is no necessity in the sign as such; any sign will do, if it only sets the term apart for its identification, in which this separateness ends. We should not speak of signs as "different" from each other, for difference has no place in pure Logic, which is the domain of identity, an identity made clear by signs and their transitory separation.

Order is absolute. Order of identity is all-comprehensive. Order is therefore beyond exclusion and opposites, it can not be itself excluded by Not-order. There is nothing outside of order. We may state a pseudo-beyond and call it "disorder" or "chaos." But these words have no logical meaning, disorder being neither a fact nor a thought, but merely the vague recognition of order's exclusivity. If we recognize nevertheless a beyond to order, something "to be ordered," then we introduce a non-logical entity, a disorderly matter which somehow has to be brought under the spell of order, has to be "persuaded" as Plato said, or forced into order, and it is for this material world that Logic becomes "normative," losing its purity and its all-comprehensive absoluteness. Here we are then faced with a multitude of orders, each one of them "somehow absolute" and therefore defying any unification with other orders. Order-systems, paradoxical in their plurality, can not be united by identity; their attempted unity will remain vague, "confused," and the Schoolmen will speak in such cases rather of "analogy" than of identity. A plurality of order-systems, each one of them rejecting an overarching unity, can only loosely be related: a plurality of "Being" can only vaguely be united by the improper relation of analogy. Just as the relation of exclusion was improper and only transitional, a preparation for a higher unity, so also analogy should be regarded as transitional and preparatory, and it should be restricted to those realms in which a full understanding cannot be achieved. In the religious field, where the infinite is only vaguely understood as an unfamiliar order-structure and can be brought only into a loose comparison to the familiar order of finitude such an analogy may be permitted as a preparation for a more profound insight, and so analogy was rightly used in the formation of order-structures concerning knowledge and action, in dogmas and rituals, using finite analogical expressions as a preparation for entering into the infinite Divine order.[13]

The normative and analogical aspect of Order points to a world which is not merely logical. We have to cope with this world which will throw order and logic into the subordinate role of an "organon." But subordinate or not, order and logic remain fundamental and should not be regarded as devices which touch only lightly on reality or even falsify it, a view held by Bergson and some existentialists. What this first chapter should make clear beyond doubt is the fundamental metaphysical character of fact and order, order being the most absolute and all-comprehensive fact. That this fact includes process is another important insight, not to be ignored and of decisive value on every stage of our analysis, even at the last, where personality will be revealed as structure and process in unity. Thus order stands out as a scaffold or model of reality. What may be regarded as specifically characteristic in this first phase is the prevalence of the factual over the processual element, process being swallowed up by the expanded fact of the order structure. It is fact which triumphs here; the dignity and stability of order and Logic rely on the absoluteness and necessity of their factual unity. This factual necessity is so strong that no weaker factor can break into the system, no mere "possibility" can find a place besides necessity in this order-structure. We have to reject the idea of a "logical possibility," for there is only logical necessity. Possibility will have to be faced in the very different context of mathematical order to which our next chapter will be devoted.[14]

Because of its factual necessity Order had to be discussed in this first chapter, predominantly concerned with the analysis of fact. A rigid factual order, firm in the identity of its structure, has stamped its mark on Western philosophy and science. Greek culture worshipped Order as "Dike" or "Ananke" and even as "Tyche." When process tried to free itself from its enclosure in the rigid structure of a factual necessity, it was again and again subdued and was allowed to live on only in the frame-work of a fateful order. Although the Greek genius repeatedly broke out of the narrow fences of its order and rebelled in Mythology and Tragedy against the iron law of fate, the rule of a lawful necessity was always restored. Even in the social realm, in the life of the people, the atom and the atomic structure of order prevailed, leaving their mark on the whole Western civilization, and making our society into what it is. God, at last, had to assume the character of a fact, isolated and opaque, or He had to find expression in the necessity of an order-structure: a first cause or a system. The living God of the Bible rarely found support by Western thinkers, with the exception perhaps of Heraclitus and Aristotle, the Logos and the Prime Mover. But even their insights had to undergo a decisive interpretation in medieval and post-medieval time in order to reach and develop the full truth of a reality beyond mere order.

Yet, the metaphysical importance of fact and order should not be minimized. To be sure, fact and order are predominantly abstract. Process as self-limiting thought is subordinated to a stability of structure. But this emphasis on structure is not an arbitrary reduction, it is dictated by a reality which requires thought to do what it does and which discloses through this abstracting activity its own nature in fact and order. Thought subjects itself to fact and order, and it reveals thus the reality behind abstraction, behind fact and behind order, both rendered objective and absolute through the self-effacement of thought.

II. FUNCTION AND INFINITY

Identity and Order, the two pillars of Logic, were grounded in "fact" and "process." Their paradoxical unity was the essential feature in this realm. In its tension it gave rise to another not less baffling paradox: Order, identity is a "oneness," but in this oneness a "many" is contained, a manifold of terms which however, is absorbed and disappears in the oneness, and because of this absorption does not become a problem for investigation in this realm. Order is here understood as one structure, a factual and processual unity, which as a "structuring" contains its many terms.

It is here that Metaphysics proceeds by entering in and developing the riddles of one and many, passed by in the logical realm, where they came to the fore in a rudimentary manner only. In fact, the logical relation of identity is itself a riddle, contradictory in its structure, a togetherness which falls apart, a separateness which appears as unity. In any case, a higher unity is wanted which justifies the separation as well as the unification and for which the relational structure is only an intermediate stage. Such a higher unity would be neither a mere structure of relativity nor a process, neither a fact, closed and limited, nor a procedure in need of such facts. We have to assume such a unity as the ground of the relational, an "absolute," even if it does not lend itself to a clear outlining by abstraction. It is enough, if the working of such an absolute, of such a ground, can be recognized, and, indeed, such working is to be found in that field of abstraction which we are entering now: The field of mathematical operation and its products.

Mathematics has often been identified with Logic, although both realms are very different: For it is only in the mathematical operation that the absolute ground is at work and forces the narrow static structure of identical order into flux. Only here an entity is at work which breaks the relational structure apart and separates the facts from their process; only here, therefore, the process is detached as a "one" from the "many" facts which as many remain separate over against the process and are not absorbed in identity, although they are still embedded in the process. Only here, and not at another stage, does "possibility" arise, as a new and complex medium which has "necessity" over and against it, both, possibility and necessity, in need of each other and both in their separation and unification manifesting a common ground which as such is neither only possible nor only necessary, but "real," although this reality is hidden at this abstract stage. The terms or facts are now many possible terms of the one necessary process; but, on the other hand, the process is only a possibility with regard to its terms which build it up and thus are necessities for the process. That here possibility and necessity are found as well in the terms as in the process, is a paradox which points to the mysterious ground, in which both possibility and necessity vanish. The mutual interaction of terms and process is seen furthermore in that the terms as many will seem to enclose the process, swallow it in their factual plurality which now as a loose unity, as a processual "summing up," will give rise to the complex facts, called "sums"; but at the same time these sums will be swallowed in their turn by the process, will open up, as carried in the processual flux, to ever new sums, every one possible only and relative. It is evident that in this growing and advancing process the sums are not "identical," but show the advance in being at different stages in the process. But, in spite of this, the sums are, wherever they close up, possibilities of one and the same process. We are accustomed to call this complex unity of difference and sameness an "equality," and the process by which this equality is built up, the process of "equation." The sums are possibles in the equating process; they "are" not so much equal as that they proceed as possibles in the process of equation.

The facts which in this way proceed as sums in the advancing equation are called "numbers" or "aggregates." They are what they are only in the process of numbering, only as possibles, as "functions" in the process. The advancing process as such is appropriately called a "method" which means literally a "way," a way of operation. Numbers are not facts in the sense of atoms closed in isolation, nor in the sense of order-systems, similarly closed and exclusive. They proceed over against a process, and the facts as well as the process are mutually constitutive, possible and necessary respectively. It is the ground which is responsible for this complexity, the "Absolute" beyond the relativity of operation, and it will now be appropriate to approach, as far as it is possible, this hidden ground of absoluteness. Such an approach is the more important as modern Mathematics has made this ground its central problem and has discovered a multitude of new forms, rising out of this ground. It is the mathematical "Infinite" which as an inexhaustible creative ground has become the fundamental problem of mathematical inquiry. It is not only that the numbers or aggregates are in their advance determined by the Infinite towards which they rise,—every number receives this Infinite into its boundaries and is, as the Pythagoreans already knew, as well finite as infinite, as well definite as indefinite. There is, however, no "infinite number" as such, nor is there any infinite operation. Infinity is no predicate, nor does it lend itself to predication: It is therefore neither quantitative nor qualitative, although it has been interpreted in both ways. It is neither a possibility nor a necessity, modalities which belong to number and process respectively. The Infinite can be grasped only in its influence on the numbers, in the way in which it conveys its own absoluteness to the relativity of the numbers, the sums, every one in its factual and processual nature relative as well as absolute. We have a special term for the reflex of absoluteness on the mathematical sum: We call such a sum a "Whole." Every number or aggregate is a whole, and by this wholeness we mean an absoluteness which is only conferred from beyond on an entity which is essentially relative, not absolute, and which proceeds in relation to other sums. Numbers, under the impact of Infinity, consummate the process of operation in their sum, but at the same time the process is allowed to advance beyond this consummation, revealing the Whole as being also a "Part" of ever other wholes. Numbers are as well wholes as parts, a paradox which originates in the fact that the wholeness is due to a higher power, entering the relativity of the mathematical sphere and conveying something of this higher sphere, its absoluteness, to the relational facts. In this way every whole has infinite possibilities in its parts, but every part has equally infinite possibilities as to the whole, and so the mathematician Cantor, concerned with the mystery of Infinity, discovered the nature of "infinite aggregates" as having an equal power (Maechtigkeit), whether they are parts or wholes.[1]

The ambiguous role which the whole plays under the impact of infinity baffled even Kant who rightly detected absoluteness in the whole, in "totality," but who got involved in antinomies as long as he identified totality and absoluteness, omitting the power of Infinity. When he rediscovered this power, he understood that totality is sought for only as total and merely appears as absolute through Infinity, yielding therefore its absoluteness to ever other wholes as parts in a relativising operation. Wholeness has under the disguise of "Perfection" fooled many thinkers into believing that it has an absoluteness of its own, although it is dependent on an infinite power which throws perfection in spite of its seeming absoluteness into finitude and relativity.[2]

Infinity bears a negative name, but it has essentially a positive influence, absolutising the facts in the operation of numbering. The positive influence was overlooked by Empiricists who explained Infinity as a deficiency of the psyche, an impotence of the human mind to stop the process. Infinity is no impotence and no psychological fact. In its light indeed the processes of abstraction and their facts show their limitation, their deficiency, but the Infinite itself is not deficient. It will reveal its positive power on every stage of our investigation as more and more creative, entering step by step deeper into the core of our factual world. There is a negative element, indeed, in Mathematics, but it is to be looked for in the numbers themselves which carry a nought with them in the equating process in so far as they fail on their way to Infinity to ever realize it, remaining possibilities, functions only in the process. The nought therefore is in the making of every number just as the Infinite is, so that numbers seem to proceed between Nought and Infinity, as if they were a product of "Zero" and "infinity." When Newton explained his "fluxion-theory," he spoke of numbers as coming into existence only in order to vanish on the road to Infinity, disappearing into nothing and restored again under the impact of Infinity. It is not a matter of chance that the two mathematicians, Descartes and Pascal, when trying to characterize the human situation, used the insight which numbers provide, and placed man between Nothingness and Infinity.

Numbers proceed through Nought and Infinity. A certain irreality has therefore darkened the mathematical realm. Thus Plato ranked Mathematics between the illusion of the cave and the fully lighted reality of reason. There is an elusive quality about the facts of mathematics which have meaning only in the process of their operation. There is not number as such and apart from it the operation of numbering, as if the latter could be just as well omitted. The operation and construction is the essence of the number, numbers are what they do, their possibility is their being.[3] The "infinite aggregate" of Cantor is a fact, to be sure, but a fact which presents itself, as all sums do, in the form of a procedure. Such facts seem to slip away in an infinite progress and regress;[4] their processual involvement is so important that ever new ways of this involvement had to be discovered, starting with addition, multiplication, division, but advancing to many other more complex explorations with regard to the possibilities residing in numbers. We may call these various ways of exploring numbers and their possibilities "mathematical dimensions," using here a term which we are accustomed to use in the spatio-temporal realm, where dimensions reflect the various possible operations with regard to things and events. The dimensional operations characterize also the numbers involved, not only the method, the process of operation itself. Ever new numbers have been discovered together with ever new methods as dimensional expressions of the number-realm. Modern mathematics has long ago surpassed a restriction to integers, faced with ever new number- and method-discoveries. The close affinity between these various numbers and their methods is so strong that their unity, welded together under the impact of Infinity, should not be destroyed by tearing the number from its method in order to better understand both. Whenever this is done, number as well as method lose their meaning and appear as arbitrary inventions of the intellect, a game played by the mind. The complaint directed against mathematics that it is a whimsical game and nothing more, has been the result of such an unwarranted divorce between number and method. It is a symptom of immaturity to tear apart in order to understand. The broken pieces will defy any insight. Primitive man thus isolated number, gazed at it and was terrified by what seemed to him a sinister power, with which he tried to cope by magic.

The infinite possibility, residing in number, has led to the idea of "density." Density expresses the infinite possibility working in number and operation. Numbers are "dense," because infinite other numbers can be drawn out of any sum, and infinite other numbers can be found between numbers advancing in the process. This infinite density has been termed "Continuity." But the term "continuous" should be reserved for the very different realm of space-time where we will have to discuss it. A series of numbers is dense, but not continuous. And just as density was inadequately identified with continuity, so also was the mathematical operation at times confused with the very different process which we call "Motion." Motion indeed, has to be dismissed from the number-realm, although the Pythagoreans spoke of the "self-moving number" and compared it to the soul and its motion. Motion presupposes time, but the arithmetical operation is no temporal event. The man who is involved in arithmetics, the mathematician, counts and adds, divides and thus operates in time, but this psychic phenomenon is not the mathematical operation as such, it merely follows in time the track of a timeless operation. There is neither time presupposed in Arithmetic, nor space presupposed in Geometry. The former may be more easily granted than the latter. Sums are surely not extended in time nor are we interested in the magnitude of duration that an arithmetical formula takes. But geometrical figures seem indeed to take their place in space and to assume a certain extension or magnitude. But here again we have to distinguish between the true geometrical "construction" which is the operation in the geometrical field, and the drawing which a geometrician may make on paper or on a black-board. The figures which are drawn in space are indeed extended objects but they only exemplify the abstract and un-spatial figure which is constructed out of un-extended, "mathematical points," and no aggregate of unextended points could ever result in an extension. The geometrical figures are not more extended than arithmetical formulas are. If this were not so, then Analytic Geometry would be unable to express the geometrical figure in arithmetical formulas. The geometrical figure is nothing but a rule of construction, a fact in operation, just as number is. That some Geometrical patterns can be applied in space is true, and shows that there is a connection between mathematics and the spatio-temporal realm. We have taken account of this by using the term dimension in both fields. But the discovery of the various Non-Euclidian Geometries, some of which are not applicable to space, should have made it clear that the realm of Geometry as such is rigidly separated from the spatial realm, and that the term "geometrical space" is a misnomer, just as "arithmetical time" would be.

After having ruled out time and space and extension there still remains a specific mathematical medium to be strongly emphasized, the medium of Infinity. Infinity is responsible for the creative ventures in the mathematical field. This Infinity is irrational, opaque, not caught in any abstract device, neither in number nor in figure, and only dimly seen in the density of the mathematical facts, giving rise to an abundance of dimensional operations and their corresponding elements. It is this Infinity which separates Mathematics definitely from pure Logic, a separation which has recently been blurred. But it is not space and time which have entered the mathematical field, and any interpretation which regards mathematics as abstracted from the spatio-temporal experience of things, of material objects, is a form of naive realism, and misses the specific character of the mathematical sphere. Mathematics is indeed not as pure as Logic is, for the medium which has entered abstraction here and confuses it, is the enigmatic Infinity, a medium which unquestioned but also unelucidated, assumes the dominating role. The irrational nature of Infinity was recognized already by the Greeks, who, with the exception of the Pythagoreans, abhorred Infinity as hostile and detrimental to rational abstract thought and which could only be expressed by a negative term. Even Aristotle placed the Infinite in the realm of what he regarded a diminished reality, the realm of the Potential, a realm which we will discuss in a later chapter of this work and which will open the problems of life. Thus, indeed, Infinity points ahead beyond abstraction to a richer realm. But before we reach this realm with its new insights and problems, we have to follow step by step the road of abstraction itself, and so we have to enter now a level of abstraction where the Infinite assumes a wider meaning and a more conspicuous power, and reveals itself as the "Given."

III. EXTENSION, SUBSTANCE AND CAUSALITY

Infinity, closed to abstraction but instrumental in operation and in density, gave to the mathematical realm and to its elements a complex and highly imaginative character. There is an ingenious touch to everything which the mathematician discovers, a richness absent in pure Logic. Mathematical operations and constructions were often compared to artistic creations because of the creative source of the Infinite. Because of this strange and inexplicable medium Mathematics moves away from Logic and prepares abstraction for a confrontation with Infinity, more conspicuous and powerful, "given" to abstraction and thus affecting the elements of abstraction in a radical way. While the infinite medium of Mathematics does not ever come as such into focus but is apparent only in the inexhaustibility of operation and in the density of its elements, the medium of Infinity is now "given," present to abstraction. Abstraction can not state more than just this giveness, and the way in which the given is faced asks for a special expression, vague and tentative: "Intuition," a term with which not much more is said than that no abstract thinking is involved.[1]

Mathematics approached the Infinite by a negative term, because it surpasses rational elucidation. That also the intuitively Given is beyond abstract reason, is obvious, and thus it too, surpasses any predication: no attribute can be attached to the Given, and it shows its paradoxical nature in the way in which it is given "to" abstraction, relative to the operations and facts of abstraction, although it is essentially absolute, not relative. In spite of being given to abstraction, it rejects therefore any enclosure into a rational pattern.

But as "given" to abstract thought it asks for a positive term, no mere negation does justice to its presence. We may call it the "ground" or the absolute medium or the "space-time-given," for it will indeed be responsible for the features we are confronted with in space and time. But when we try to interpret it as order or as function, we miss its nature. It defies both patterns and remains aloof to all the operations, to all the goings-on which abstraction builds on its ground. And if we regard it as a "ground," we must confess that it is a ground which rejects the surface-happenings which pass over it just as much as it supports them. It is indifferent to all facts and processes, closed to operations and constructions, opaque in every regard except its "givenness." Its indifference to abstraction and its elements is the only attribute we can possibly attach to it. And so abstraction will indeed limit its insight with regard to the given to this one attribute: its indifference to abstraction. For abstraction can not go beyond its own sphere and thus it can get hold of this message from another world only in so far as it views it from its own perspective, only taking in the effect which it has on its own operation. Because of this limited perspective we may speak here of "abstract space-time," distinguishing it from "lived space-time" which will be discussed at a later stage. But although termed "abstract space-time" it is not really an abstraction; it is rather closed to abstraction, for it is the mysterious ground of the infinite Given.

What we can grasp, therefore, with regard to this Given is just its closedness to abstraction and nothing more, its closedness to operation and to any kind of division, to one and to many. It may appear because of this closedness as "empty," but empty only with regard to those functions in which abstraction is interested. Space-time is empty because it rejects all operation and maintains itself against the functions which proceed on its ground. The power of maintaining its integrity is thus the only attribute which abstraction can possibly detect in the Given as untouched by operation and division. This attribute will be conceived by abstraction as "indivisibility." But again, such a negative term does not do full justice to the positive nature of the Given, and so a term will have to be found which expresses the positive character, the power of maintaining itself against division. This term is the "continuous," space-time is continuous. Cointinuity has been much discussed in the history of thought, but has remained a problem, evidently so, for it characterizes the enigmatic Given. Continuity expresses the positive power of maintaining unity against division. Divisibility enters into continuity only in order to be rejected. When Aristotle defined the continuous as divisible, infinitely divisible, although not actually divided, this definition was criticized heavily and with good reason: for what is divisible will sooner or later be actually divided. The continuity of space-time can not possibly mean this. The continuity of the infinite medium, of the space-time-given means really that it maintains its essentially indivisible character and rejects any kind of division.[2]

What abstraction grasps in the Given is this: its continuity; it can not go beyond this insight. It cannot even state whether the Given has the nature of a fact or of a process, whether it should be called a factual "continuum" or a processual "continuity." Nor can abstraction attribute to the Given the character of necessity, although mythology, attracted by the mystery of the Given, has indeed regarded it as a power of necessity, of "Fate," a fate untouched by the happenings in its orbit. Mythology has even gone further and has interpreted the rejection and closure against the surface-happenings as a hostility, a fiendish power which disturbs and crushes the things unfolding under its rule: Chronos, the demon of Time, devours his own children, and even Aristotle regards time as the medium in which things degenerate and pass away. But Metaphysics has to be more cautious in its statements, it can emphasize only the aloofness and undisturbed continuity of the space-time-given, an aloofness and indifference which will however affect the events in its orbit. These events, unlike the facts in the number-process, will not merely be possibles in an equating operation, loosely connected in series of sums: they will, on the one hand, stand out from one and the same ground as equal in their structure, levelled down to indifferent entities upon an indifferent ground, to mere "here-nows," each one nothing but just a "here-now." On the other hand, these here-nows will under the impact of continuity merge into each other, not as loose sums containing their processual articulation, but compact wherever grasped; and so it will seem as if the operation is accompanied by an indivisibility which "extends" with the factual entities and fulfills to any "extent" the indivisible character of the Given. We speak indeed with regard to any such extended here-now of its "extension" which is continuous, that is indivisible although it lends itself to a manifoldness which it grounds as well as rejects, itself, in spite of the manifold, an indivisible "one," an indivisible "here-now," fulfilling to its extent the total nature of the here-now. Wherever we detect a here-now, we are faced with the full here-now, expressing in its extent space-time as such. There is not, as Kant thought, a division into parts building together a whole, similar to a sum in the number-realm. Wherever a here-now is present, it absorbs the full indivisible space-time, is the here-now as absolute. But after having stated this with all the necessary emphasis, we must concede, that every here-now is only to an "extent" the here-now and that it fits, in extending, to any event or even plurality of events and things and is in so far open to a manifold. The paradoxes involved in extension are the result of the impact of the Given, and so it is not astonishing that extension has played a dubious role in the history of thought. It is not even possible to discriminate with regard to extension, in how far it is a fact or a process, in how far it is an extended factual entity or an extending processual unit, thus again repeating the ambiguity of the Given.

And here another point has to be emphasized: it is not the ground, not the Given as such, not space-time itself which is extended, only the operational elements are. Not time has extension in duration, but events have. Not space is extended in breadth and length, but facts are. The underlying ground sheds only its indivisibility and indifference into the surface-sphere and welds the elements of this sphere together in extension, into the here-now and holds them in the unity of an unbroken continuity, allowing however the semblance of an articulation in so far as the extending process accompanies and welds together what, at the same time, seems factually to be closed off to any "extent." The continuity of the extended realm of things and events is, therefore, not the same as the continuity of the ground. The ground was continuous in the sense of maintaining indivisibility against any division; the "extension" is continuous in as much as it maintains indivisibility, but allows any "extent" to come to a stop as if it were absolute in itself, stretching however beyond this very extent in an all-comprehensive union. What makes us distinguish "places" in the continuous extension is the double aspect of the here-now, separating as well as uniting, known already to Aristotle. The here-now extends and welds to an unbroken unity and fulfillment of space-time as such; but the here-now separates also by closing off any extent of unity, equally a fulfillment of space-time, wherever found. It is this stretching and closing and stretching again which has the semblance of an articulation of places, each one necessary as well as possible, absolute as well as relative. The ambivalence of the here-now as process and as fact causes the twofold character of unity and plurality. Extension is, indeed, as Plato saw, a "hybrid" concept. Extension stretches as a process and closes off as a fact, and so it seems as if every closed here-now reached to another here-now, the here to a there, the now-before to a now-after. As far as extension emphasizes the process, it is one; as far as it stresses the factual, it appears as many; but both are only aspects of the same. Therefore the processual extension will give account of its places as a "measuring" process, and the places in their turn will assume in the measurement a "magnitude," measurement and magnitude building each other mutually in a tighter union than numbers and numbering did. We call this measuring of magnitude a "dimension," and just as the mathematical dimensions were concerned with numbers, so these dimensions are concerned with events and things. We used the term "dimension" in the mathematical field, but its model belongs to space-time, and its literal meaning is "measurement." There is a difference, however, between the dimensional operations in the number-realm and those in the field of extension: In mathematics the operation, although linked to its facts, is over against these facts; but in the dimensional space-time-extension the processual and factual elements are really one, the here-now being an extending process as well as an extended fact. If nevertheless the emphasis should be directed to the one or the other under neglect of its counterpart, practical considerations, not metaphysical insights are at stake. For the practical task of measuring the process will be emphasized, and when this happens the time-extension will come to the fore, while an emphasis on the factual magnitude will isolate the spatial extension: Thus "time as such" will appear separate from "space as such." But this seeming independence of both has meaning only for practical purposes which indeed are essential in daily life as well as in scientific investigations, so that the separate consideration of space and of time will assume a fundamental attitude. The unity of both will be restored, however, not only when metaphysical considerations enter, but even with regard to measurement itself: for the temporal magnitudes will be measured by spatial distances, and spatial magnitudes by temporal stretches.

The immense importance of the dimensional sphere, of measurement and magnitude, will make us oblivious with regard to the indivisibility of extension and with regard to the ground, the Given. But this indivisible medium will be rediscovered, whenever man pierces beneath the surface and seeks a deeper truth. It is the mystic who has again and again reminded man of the ground beneath the turmoil of life's operations. So Spinoza rediscovered the indivisibility, underlying extension and gave it Divine character; and the "Now" as indivisible was hailed by mystics who imbued it with eternal absoluteness and contemplated this Now not only in its all-comprehensive unity as a Divine presence, but also in its character as "instant," indivisible and eternal too.

Measurement and magnitude play a dominant role in life and in Science, and so it seems as if the Given had exhausted its power in the medium of extension and its articulated infinity. There is a temptation for the scientist to reduce the Given to extension as to the main object of his interest. Descartes, the mathematician, did just this; for him extension was the ultimately Given and he called it Substance. But "Substance" is not just extension, and so Descartes had to add to it another substance, the substance of thought, and he had to raise beyond these two substances a third, a Divine substance which rendered the other two to dependent entities. Substance is, indeed, more than extension and thought; the Given is not exhausted by these functions, its main character is resistance against the operation as a surface-phenomenon, it is aloofness and closure. It is this resistance, this maintenance on the part of the Given which is grasped by abstraction and is reflected in the operational elements which in their turn seem to resist, standing out from the ground, maintaining themselves against the ground, closed off, opaque and indivisible beneath the surface of a dimensional extension. They seem to resist not only with regard to the ground, but also against their sliding over into each other, against the "extending" as a process of operation. Substance is this shutting out and upholding of integrity; it is not "oneness" nor "unity," but rather closure, concentration, maintenance, opacity which characterize the enigmatic "substance." For no other elucidation of substance is possible. The substance or, as we may call it, the "thing" is a ground, closed in itself. The mysterious Given has shed its darkness into it. When Locke confessed that substance was something "I do not know what" he was right.

But we cannot stop even here: Substance is indivisible, factual, unelucidated, absolute. It is, however, also extended and as extended it carries an articulation, a relational pattern not only as an **internal** structure, but also as a structure which extends beyond the boundaries of the substance, relating this absolute thing to other absolute things. Substance is on the one hand a closed fact, absolute and isolated, without distinctions and indivisible. But Substance is in spite of its absolute isolation, also open and related, and this openness and relatedness is "inherent" in the Substance. "Inherence" is a vague term; it expresses the paradox that the relatedness "is" not itself the substance, but is only "had" by the substance. The substance "is" absolute, but "has" relatedness. What this "having" means in contradistinction to "being" must now be analyzed; Numbers "are" relational and "are" possibles as such, this is their essential nature. But substance is essentially absolute and, as it "has" only its relation, we speak of this relatedness as of an "accident" of the substance. But the substance has this accidental character necessarily: there are no substances without accidents. We are obviously here confronted by a paradox similar to that of the here-now, a similarity which shows again that substance and extension are both the result of the impact which the given ground has on the elements of operation. Just as the here-now was an indivisible here-now, absolute in its comprehensive presence, but at the same time "articulated" into here-nows which did not break up the indivisibility, so the substance is an absolute and indivisible entity, but necessarily articulated in accidental relations. The essential indivisibility and absoluteness of the substance yields to as well as holds out against a relatedness which seems to destroy it and to subject it to a necessity beyond its isolation, so that the substance is torn into a process of operation, in which it is in danger of losing its character. But Substance resists not only the ground from which it stands out, it resists also the changes to which its own relatedness condemns it, and which, although destructive, seem to sleep in the depth of the substance in order to be awakened. What adds the last and most confusing touch to this whole sphere is, however, that these very relations, although "had" only by the substance and destructive to its substantial absoluteness, provide the only knowledge which we have with regard to substances. Only these "accidents" are open to our understanding, while the substance as such remains a fascinating and at times frightening riddle. Deprived of any knowledge with regard to the substances as such, our knowledge of these relations leaves us lastly dissatisfied and may be regarded with Plato as mere "opinion," but not, as Plato thought, because it is sense-knowledge—for this would mean a shifting from metaphysics to psychology—but because it is a fragmentary knowledge of accidents only.

But is it a knowledge of accidents only? We may look at the relatedness of the substance as an accident. But it is more: the substance "has" not only the relation, it "is" also the relatedness when seen from a different angle, and it is this different angle which makes us call the Substance a "Cause." Every cause is a substance, a closed and absolute fact, to be sure. Whether we consider a thing or a situation or an idea as cause, it has first to be a closed fact, a substance in order to serve as a cause. But this granted, the cause is not only isolated and absolute, it is also essentially open and related to its "effect." We can think of a substance without having its accidents in mind, but we can not think of a cause apart from its effect. We may use our language loosely and point to a cause as "having" an effect, but what we mean is that the cause "is" the openness to its effect and in spite of being its own necessity is also a possibility. As a possibility the cause is drawn into the necessity of an operation, not unlike the way in which numbers were drawn into their operation, as a manifestation of their very nature.

Thus all the paradoxes of abstraction abound in the substance as cause. It is isolated but in relation; it is absolute, an all-comprehensive here-now, but it is in a specific way open to another here-now. This relation can be regarded as "absolute equality"; cause and effect are absolutely equal. We met this absolute equality as a paradox in the number-realm, and so its return may help here to clarify the nature of causality. The equality of numbers was grounded in the medium of Infinity which, although hidden, made every number absolute as a whole besides leaving it relative as a part in the operation of numbering. In the substantial sphere of causality Infinity has, however, entered fully into the events and is substantially "given" in them. It is because of this that it provides every factual entity with an absoluteness **not at the side** of its relativity, but **in** its very relativity. The cause is not a whole in one respect and a part in another, it is in the same respect as well whole as part; it is, like the here-now, everywhere the full whole although articulated in equality and relation. What in the mathematical realm was detectable only with regard to the "infinite aggregates": that the part had the same power (Maechtigkeit) as its whole,[3] is here present and obvious in every cause: every cause expresses the given infinity of substance, and so every cause has the full power, even if it is observed as a "part-cause" only, and this power is not as in the aggregates, a mere equivalence of correspondence between elements, detectable in a process of operation, it is immediately given in the substantial cause which as a part-cause has the full power of the whole cause. Every time, therefore, when a part-cause, a "condition" is observed, its power is that of the whole cause, it provides the necessity of the whole cause and allows to rest in it as in a fulfillment of substantiality. We may hold the conditions, as parts, apart from each other and equally so the consequences, summing them up as parts into wholes; and we may similarly relate the cause and the effect as mere parts to each other; but what we must realize, besides, is that the cause as well as the effect is an indivisible substantial whole, and that wherever we are faced with either of them, even only a part, it has the power of the whole and is thus fully necessary in spite of being also a possible.

This paradoxical phenomenon for which the infinite Given is responsible is of utmost practical importance: It enables the scientist to find in every instance of observation "the" cause, "the" causal certainty; and although the scientist is aware that such an instance of observation is only a part-condition, he feels free to use these part-conditions as full explanations of the cause and the part-consequences which he observes as the full expression of the effect. If this were not so and if the scientist had to gather "all conditions" and "all consequences" and had to wait with any statement of causal necessity until he was in the presence of these totalities, he would never come to grips with any law-statement, for such a totality can not be observed. But, in fact, the Given allows every single condition, every single part, to be the whole; and so the scientist can close his experience in causal necessity and can come to rest in systematic law.

The paradox of the whole and the part had, however, also a disastrous influence: Besides being of great advantage in its practical use, it has confused the philosophical thinking and has involved the philosopher in the so-called "infinite regress." Unable to realize that every part-cause "is" the whole cause, and that every part-effect "is" the whole effect, philosophers have believed that as every cause turns out to be the effect of another cause, and every effect the cause of another effect, no cause as such and no effect as such could really be acknowledged, and although hunted backwards and forwards in infinity the ever slipping-away causes and effects seemed to fool the thinker and to reveal ultimately that there was no real cause nor effect anywhere to be found, in which the thinker could come to rest. But this infinite regress is an illusion born out of the impotence to realize the paradoxical nature of the "cause." Just as extension, the here-now, was complete wherever it was met, just as we are in the full presence of space and time wherever there is a space and a time, so we are also faced by the cause and the whole cause wherever a condition presents itself. Every condition and every group of conditions "is" the necessity and totality of a systematic fulfillment. Of course, every system is again a part of a greater system, but this does not preclude the character of systematic totality with regard to any causally interrelated whole. There is no reason to dismiss the system as a merely expedient and arbitrary device, as if it hid the fact that we do not really have any system and any necessary totality at all. But there is still less reason to deify the system, as the Stoics did, and it is certainly not appropriate to bring God into the picture as the "first cause" in order to stop the infinite regress: Every cause is a first cause, as every effect is a last effect, because the nature of abstraction, of substance and operation, allows us under the impact of the Given, to stop in every stage as an absolute fulfillment.

Before ending this chapter, the question may be broached whether extension, substance, cause, and their ground, the Given, are "a-priori-entities" or not. The distinction between a priori and a posteriori is sanctioned by the thought of great minds, but it is vague and based on psychological grounds, on the absence or presence of sensation. The findings of this chapter are obviously not as pure as those of Logic: Already mathematics presupposed a medium which was not fully lightened by abstraction, the Infinite. The Given as the ground of extension, substance, and cause is still more removed from the lucidity of Logic. But, on the other hand, neither the Given, nor extension, substance or cause are "a posteriori," if this means sense-experience. Sensation as a body-function should not be in the foreground of metaphysical discussions. The human body and its functions will have their place, when life, consciousness, appearance and imagination will be at stake, and their information will indeed as a material become an "a posteriori"-content of the "a priori"-structures which we have discussed in the preceding chapter. The Given, extension, substance and cause can not be derived from sensing: they are definitely not "a posteriori experience."

IV. CONCEPT, LAW AND PURPOSE

The ingression of the Given into the realm of abstraction resulted in paradoxical tensions all over the field. Numbers and aggregates were levelled down into the indifference of mere "here-nows"; but at the same time these indifferent entities assumed a closedness and factual isolation as absolute substances which, to complicate matters, were in spite of their absolute isolation drawn into a relatedness, into causal flux, and this causal flux seemed to destroy their substantiality, landing them in the illusion of the infinite regress. We may concentrate on the closedness and stable presence of the substance, fulfilling in its isolation the here-now and assuming the character of the whole, the cause, the effect in its totality. But we may also concentrate instead on the indistinctness of the extent, the gliding of the here into the there, the now-before into the now-after, and on the accidental relatedness of substances to each other, destroying the necessity of the substance in possibilities which come no-where to rest. Each view is, however, incompatible with the other. If we rely on the former, we emphasize the necessity and stability of our world: we are scientists and feel secure in the firm framework of abstraction. If we drift, however, into the second perspective, we acknowledge nothing but "matter of fact," nothing but the accidental sequence and togetherness which may or may not be stopped anywhere and which provides no necessity to rest in.

The astonishing fact is that both views are held simultaneously by most people and that, although each one is incompatible with the other, our common-sense attitude is in no way disturbed by this glaring inconsistency. We indulge in the security of a tight and stable necessity, totally determined and totally understood in every one of its elements, and therefore we worship a Science which provides us with the comfort of a secure and predictable life. But on the other hand, we allow this same world to be loosely knit, offering in every moment infinite possibilities, perpetually changing and unpredictable, enjoyed or feared according to our temperament and situation. When we awaken from time to time out of this muddle of attitudes, we are struck by their incompatibility and haunted by the incompleteness of each of them, and we become positivists with regard to Science and Skeptics with regard to life.

But when we look more closely, we find that this incompatibility was already foreshadowed in every finding of abstraction and only brought to a head in the confrontation with the Given. What after all was the mysterious fact, constituted by the process of thought but absorbing this thought in the "expanded fact" of Order? What after all were the mathematical facts, over against their process of operation, expressing as wholes the infinite medium, but "parting" from each position and assuming another part-position in the infinite medium? When fact, in its absoluteness and closed opacity, at last separated itself from all operations and withdrew into the mystery of the Given, its impact on the operations, in spite of its withdrawal, resulted in an abundance of paradoxes, of extension, of substances and accidents, of causes and effects. Extension, substance and causality expressed the power of the Given at the mercy of which these elements of abstraction had to proceed, involved in insolvable paradoxes. These paradoxes are not "psychological" difficulties of a subjective mind, they are rooted in abstraction itself, are objective incompatibilities. The procedure which abstraction finds in order to cope with these difficulties is therefore equally objective, a necessary procedure, dictated by the fundamental dialectics of abstraction itself.

It is here, in this procedure of reconciliation, that abstraction finds its most noble task and its most ingenious results. In coping with the Given, abstraction does not try to subject it to its own devices, which would result in a falsification: It directs its operation only toward this Given, recognizing it as beyond its sphere, but at the same time accepting it as the ultimate guide which, as guide and only as guide, enters into the entities of thought. Things are now tested in the light of the Given, they are not only thought, but "thought through." Not all thought runs in the track of reflection, that is of "thinking through." Fact, number, substance, and cause, extension and continuity were pre-reflective findings of thought. They have to take their place now in a process of reflective or, as we may call it, "propositional thinking," and they are in this process steps on the way toward the Given.

Propositional thought, the thought which thinks through, is concerned with the Given, directed toward the Given, "intends" the Given, to use a scholastic term. Propositions have an "intention" which points beyond their terms to something not included in the proposition, not mastered by thought, but contained nevertheless in thought as an object of intention. Reflection is dominated by this intention and it calls the object of this intention not by its mysterious name, the Given, which expresses its detachment and opacity, but by a name which reveals rather the role which the Given now plays in reflective thought: it calls it "Meaning." Meaning is that which is given but nevertheless sought for, evading enclosure in abstract terms, although it is the ultimate concern of all abstract thinking. Propositions are concerned with meaning, all their terms point to meaning, intend meaning, and it is this meaning, now openly in view, which gives a new character and ordered structure to the enigmatic and paradoxical findings of prereflective thought.

The word "Meaning" may seem vague. But we have to start with a term which although in need of more clarification, gives us a foothold and strikes us as new. For we have to be aware that the propositional realm transforms by the newness of its approach whatever we have been faced with as the result of abstraction on lower levels. What the proposition intends as its meaning is therefore neither a mere fact, nor a thing, nor can meaning be regarded as a "whole" over against the propositional terms as its parts. Furthermore: the proposition is in no causal relation to its meaning: all these terms, as fact, thing, whole, part and cause are misleading analogies when used in the propositional realm. Their reflective transformation lifts them into a different atmosphere, and this holds true especially with regard to the Given itself which as "Meaning" loses its absolute detachment, closedness and resistance, just as fact, substance and cause will lighten up and open toward an equally open meaning. Meaning enters into every term of the proposition, and so we may speak of these terms as not only intending meaning, but also as "having" meaning, they are what they are as stations on the way to meaning or, as we may now express it, on the way to "Truth." Propositions intend Truth.

What is "Truth"? It is that Given which in spite of being given is sought for, intended as meaning throughout the course of propositional thought, but caught in none of the abstract terms of the proposition. Truth is not a "thing" and it is not concerned with things. To believe that meaning and truth end in things as their ultimate aim, would be a regression to a level of abstraction we should have left behind. Truth is about more than mere things, facts, wholes etc. The difficulty is, however, that truth is not expressible in propositional terms, but only intended, so that it is impossible to give a full propositional account of truth itself. We have at this moment to be satisfied with the statement that truth is that which propositions intend as their meaning and which is as intended somehow included in the abstract structure.

Meaning dominates the propositional process. It is therefore wrong to interpret propositions according to the model which mathematical operations provide. This mistake has been committed by men like Hobbes and the logicists. Propositions only superficially take the form of an equation, but their terms are not in equation, not in any direct relation to each other. They intend meaning and converge toward the one and only meaning in which they meet as their unity. We call a term which is directed to its meaning: a "Concept." Concepts are not open to other concepts but to the meaning toward which they converge and in which they meet.

We mentioned above that meaning enters into the proposition and that it is therefore as "given" not only intended but also "had." Thus every concept is closed as **having** meaning, and open as **intending** meaning. Its having meaning can be conceived as an "anticipation," as if every concept reaching out for meaning included in its orbit all the others on the way to meaning, assuming the character not only of a fact but also of a process. In its processual aspect it may be called a "phase," because being processual itself, it takes its place in a wider process, as a "phase" in this process. That fact and process undergo a unity with each other was a phenomenon which we met on every stage of abstraction. But either the one of these elements was absorbed by the other, as process by fact on the logical level, or both remained over against each other in interaction, as number and method, and still, although closely united as cause and it's accidental operation. Here in the realm of reflective thought, however, this same paradox returns but it is elucidated in the "concept" which is itself both closed as a fact and open as a phase, and it is able to express this double-nature because meaning has entered the process and its terms, uniting both and conveying to both the character of this unification, making the process factual and the facts processual, insofar as they have and intend meaning. Through meaning the proposition itself becomes a concept and takes its place in wider processes as their phase; but on the other hand, the proposition is carried by concepts which are its phases, just as the proposition as such was a phase in a wider setting.

This complex nature of the concept as fact and as phase may be understood by the modalities of possibility and necessity which characterized the pre-reflective abstractions. Thus we may call the concept, as having meaning, a necessity, and in its character of intending meaning a possibility. But those terms do not really fit here: for the possible and the necessary are over against each other, the possible being possible for a necessity, and the necessary being necessary with regard to a possibility. Here, however, in the concept the possible and the necessary are united and are in their unity confronted by a third entity, the meaning with regard to which the concept is both, possible and necessary at once. It is therefore advisable to use specific terms: the concept is not possible as well as necessary, it is "universal" as well as "particular"; as universal it reaches out toward meaning, while as particular it anticipates this meaning and fulfills it. Thus it is phase and fact at once under the impact of meaning which is both given and sought for. Meaning elucidates and justifies concepts and it is by concepts that the Given is transformed from a bewildering and confusing opacity into a lucid meaning, achieved by "thinking through." With meaning, the Infinity of the mathematical realm and the Given of the space-time field have taken openly their place in thought, and thus the paradoxes of the whole which is open as a part, of the substance which "has" its accidents, and of the cause which "is" its own part-condition have disappeared. Every concept is an anticipation of truth and as such a whole, a substance, a cause; but it is also only an outreach and therefore a part, an accident, a condition with regard to meaning, to truth.

Universality and particularity are characteristics of concepts and only of concepts. No fact or thing as such is particular. We understand the universal together with its particularity; torn apart, the universal is as incomprehensible without the particular as is the particular without the universal. But in their unity they give an unparalleled depth and clarity of insight. We call this insight which the unity of universality and particularity conveys "difference" and it is this difference which expresses the distinct nature of things in the conceptual realm.

Differences are conceptual and reflect the double aspect of the universal and particular. When we use the term "different" in Logic and Mathematics, we have "thought these fields through" and have stated their results in concepts and propositions. Difference has the absoluteness of factual particularity, it makes the concept what it is, for a concept "is" its difference. But on the other hand, difference reaches out to other concepts and relates itself to them in its distinctness from them, it subjects itself in this relation to a wider meaning. Identity and equality were pre-reflective and, in their combination of absoluteness and relativity, enigmatic and paradoxical; but with "difference" we have entered a lightened and totally clarified realm. Furthermore: What had baffled as the paradox of substance and accident is also resolved by difference, which has an absolute "substantial" quality, but at the same time an "accidental" relational distinctness, reaching out and connecting the difference with other conceptual distinctions. It is in this way that reflective thought assumes an unparalled freedom and flexibility, for it will be allowed to stop in every distinction as in a truth, satisfactory in its anticipation of meaning, but at the same time it will be drawn forward into a process of further clarification and distinction, carrying into ever new conceptual findings. Here no illusion of an infinite regress will discourage, for the fulfillment and rest in every discovery of a clear distinction will be obvious and decisive.[1]

Particularity and universality, united in difference, are two aspects of conceptual thought, both indispensible and equally important. It is a fallacy to emphasize the one at the expense of the other, as has been done by various schools of thought. How important the particular, the "substantial" element in the concept is can be seen in the weight which the "subject" has in the propositional structure. The "subjectum" characterizes the substantial ground, the anticipation, and thus carries the propositional process in its drive, giving a definite absoluteness of unity to its terms. It has therefore been a vain attempt to eliminate or even to minimize the weight of the subject and to replace it by a merely relational order. Certainly, the subject is not only the ground of the proposition; it humbly takes its place at the side of its predications, revealing universal and relational outreach beside substantial anticipation. Thus every proposition analyzes its subject and also synthesizes it with its predicates; every proposition is both an analysis and a synthesis.

But after having stated the importance of the subject, we have to acknowledge that a onesided emphasis on it, as absolute ground, may endanger the intentional character of conceptual dynamism and neglect the equally important role of the universal. The equal importance of both in the light of meaning will even make it imperative that both be allowed to exchange their weight relative to meaning. Just as in the mathematical field possibility and necessity could, under the impact of Infinity, be thrown into number and method respectively, so here, in the service of meaning, the role of the substantial anticipation will be assumed at times by the particular subject, and at times by the universal outreach. When the latter happens, the particulars will appear as steps toward universal anticipation and will be included in its orbit. In this way the universal structure as the anticipation of truth advances to the most elevated device of conceptual thought, the "Law." Law, indeed, is an anticipation of truth; it includes its particulars in its universality, and does justice to the conceptual sphere in the way in which it builds on these particulars, and does not set itself up as a purely logical order which has absorbed its facts in a structure of identity. It has in common with logical order its dominant universal character, and so it has at times been regarded as akin to the structure of identity; [2] but it is essential for law as a conceptual structure that, unlike identity, it preserves its facts as different and rely on these facts which, as "instances," are subjected to the law, but which remain nevertheless detached and independent in their particularity. It so happens that these instances are "confirmed" by the law, but the law is "verified" by its instances. In this way law and instances need each other mutually, and it is a perversion of the truth to regard the law as "the" truth, as the only necessity in the conceptual realm divorced from its instances, and to build a system of interconnected laws as the only fulfillment of truth and meaning. Science has at times overstressed its adoration of the universality of law, and has identified its law-structure with reality as such. But even Mathematics, in its much greater independence from the Given, can not withdraw entirely into its system; by so much less can a conceptual systematization withdraw: for it is only an intention toward the Given, only a humble approach to it, perpetually reminded of its limitation by the factual instances without which the law remains only an empty shell.[3]

The instances belong to the law; they, as its possibles, are "confirmed" by the law, but as its necessities "verify" it. The essential interaction of law and its instances does not stop even here, however: Confirmation and verification illustrate the static aspect of the law, which stands in its instances as an anticipation of truth. But the law is also a phase in the conceptual process, is drawn into the dynamism of inquiry, and here the law is perpetually widened by its instances which in the process of "deduction" and "induction" fill the law with particular richness and alter it on its road toward truth. Deduction and induction can be called dimensional operations with regard to law and instances, and are as important and indispensible for them as the dimensional operations were essential for number and spatio-temporal objects. Deduction and induction are not accidentally added to law and instances: they perpetually correct both through each other. At every stage of this process the law will assume a new universality of anticipation, but it will also express a richer particularity, determined by the newly included instances which limit but also enrich it.

What we call a "Hypothesis" is such an anticipation of law, limited by its instances, but open to further instances and the correction which these instances may impose upon it. Laws, as hypothetical, are conceptual phases in the propositional process, mere steps on the road to truth.

Laws, like concepts, are anticipations of truth as well as stepping-stones on the way to truth. Truth remains an ideal which, as an intended meaning, leads on but is never fulfilled in its entirety. Truth or meaning does not lie, therefore, in concepts or laws, for these point merely toward a truth which lies beyond them. Though we may think of the ideal of truth and meaning in the manner of concept or law, universal and particular at once, the integration of these aspects would have to be so strong as to surpass the power of abstraction. Abstraction can not encompass truth within its forms, but it has found a term which, at least vaguely, points to this ideal of total universality and total individuation, and this term is "Being," Being as absolute and at times compared to Life and God.

Being has puzzled and driven philosophers to search ever since Parmenides identified it with thought, ever since Plato wooed it in mystical vision and Aristotle came to regard it as the prime object of metaphysical inquiry. It is no fact, no cause and no substance, nor is it an order, a law; neither is it subject or predicate in any proposition. Being is none of these; it stands as an ideal of meaning and truth behind all concepts, all laws, subjects and predicates. On the other hand, Being belongs to abstraction and especially to the highest level of abstraction, to the propositional sphere, because only here are truth and meaning intended. But although belonging to abstraction, "Being" itself is not abstract. We speak of concepts and laws as "being," but we should be aware that concepts and laws "have" being only insofar as they anticipated being, and they show their deficiency with regard to being precisely because they "intend" it, have a direction toward it, exhibit a tendency to become it and, in so doing show their distance from it.[4]

The extraordinary phenomenon of "Being," as intended and at the same time anticipated, demands a specific term to characterize it. This term is the "Symbol." We should use the word "Symbol" only in the propositional realm, and only with regard to "Being." Symbols are those entities of abstraction which intend a Being which they are not, and at the same time anticipate this Being, and just by so much fulfill it. In other words: Symbols, somehow anticipating a Being which they are not, will "stand for" this Being, will "represent" this Being. All concepts and laws stand for, represent, symbolize Being. In this way and only in this way symbols "are."

Being is symbolized by all concepts and laws, and appears therefore differently in every one of these symbols. But this does not justify the scholastic idea of an "analogy" of being on the reflective level. There is here only Being as such, not different kinds of Being, vaguely connected by the relation of analogy. There is only the absolute Being, the "οὐσία," but indeed the symbolizations of οὐσία, the "ὄντα," are different with regard to each other, although identical in their intention. The idea of the symbol has played a great role in modern thinking, and rightly so, but its essence has not always been grasped. At times it has been hypostatized and used as an explanation on all levels, even on the level of life, ethics and art.[5] Again it has been reduced to a device of a lower abstraction, has been explained by the devices of part and whole. The "pars pro toto"—theory is, however, misleading with regard to the symbol. The symbol cannot be reduced to any other form of abstraction, for the way in which it anticipates and at the same time merely intends

Being has no comparison on other levels, and it is just this that makes it so difficult to give a clear status to the symbol as a form. We always try to substitute some analogy drawn from a lower level, with which we are familiar, in order to feel at ease. So we speak of the symbol as a part of or as in relation to the symbolized. But the symbol is not really in a relation to Being as its "relatum." Relation connects entities of the same kind or transforms them to the same kind in order to relate them (p. 11). But Being is not of the same kind as its conceptual symbolizations and cannot be made so. The latter are as distinct concepts relative and limited, while Being is absolute and unlimited and defies any abstract formulation. Just because of this, Being is the meaning of infinite different symbolizations, intended by all of them, the truth behind every one of them. Because Being is the truth behind every one of its abstract symbols, the way is opened for us to grasp truth: it is not the case that we vainly hunt for truth, for once more the infinite regress is an illusion, and so is the "pars-pro-toto-theory" with its "part-truths" which can only be untruths. In fact, we grasp the "whole truth" in every symbol, insofar as, besides being a mere intention, it anticipates and fulfills the truth. There are symbols which anticipate to a higher degree than others, and so there is a hierarchy of symbolizations to be admitted, but that is all.[6]

Identity and equality, the essential forms of abstraction where Logic and Mathematics are at stake, have here to yield their place to "symbolization"[7] which is neither the one nor the other. Propositional thought gathers up all the lower forms of abstraction—numbers, causes, substances and accidents—thinks them through, draws them into a functional process and finally subjects them as instances to a law. In the law the propositional sphere seems to find its most comprehensive symbol, and, indeed, here is the place where scientific systematization comes to rest. But the law, as a symbol of truth, has to be understood together with its instances, hypothetical only and in need of deduction and induction in order to advance to an ever richer symbolization. On this view the particularity of the law will come most clearly into focus, when built up in the process of its instances which as stepping stones lead up to the law and are contained in the law as their fulfillment, with other words: when the law appears as the "end," the goal, and the instances as the means of this end, foreshadowing it and transparent with regard to it. In this way the unity of law and instances is more tightly bound together and reveals a new structure of abstraction, the "final cause," the "telos," as an anticipation of its means. But this final cause is not really a new structure, it is rather the cause "thought through"; and here we may grasp to the full what reflective "thinking through" means with regard to the pre-reflective devices of abstraction. What had been an opaque "cause," closed as a substance but opened in a mysterious relation, bound by absolute equality to another closed substance, the effect, both a "whole" in every one of their conditions, is now lighted up and clarified as a "final cause" which as a symbol of truth stands for the whole, anticipates this whole, carries thus its effects as means for the realization of the anticipated end and overarches as a law its instances, each one of which is meaningful with regard to the cause, predicted by it, explained by it and leading up to it as its fulfillment. The final cause is the "whole cause" because it is the symbolic anticipation and includes as such all its effects. We should, however, speak here not so much of "causes" as of "reasons," for we are moving in the sphere of conceptual thought, the final cause being a "final reason," a conceptual structure, a law. It is the law as a structure of order which replaces here the cause as a substance, a thing. That we nevertheless speak of "causes," although it is a conceptual anticipation with which we are faced here, may be explained by the fact that the final reason plays a most important role in life and action, and for this, the "action of thought" the propositional thinking through, is only a model. The final cause was therefore understood by Aristotle and other thinkers as belonging to the sphere of life, even as the ultimate principle of life itself. This is not true, however, for "anticipation" which is at the bottom of the final cause is not a specific device of life, but essential for conceptual, "intentional" thinking. From here it enters the realm of life, becomes a bridge between abstraction and the realm beyond. Indeed, it can serve as a vehicle for life and action, although it is in fact only the abstract cause "thought through."

This analysis of the final cause should not be terminated without mentioning the important influence which the anticipation of the final cause has on the pre-reflective realm of extension, of space and time. The homogeneous sequence of here-nows will, when thought through, change into conceptual phases, whereby an anticipated phase, a "telos" as the future, will be carried out in steps which as the means of this telos will realize the future, themselves phases of a "past" leading to the future as its final cause. And furthermore: the past will be gathered up in the future as a togetherness, a space-like "present," an expanded here-now. Thus there will be a double operation working in this reflected space-time, "thought through" under the aspect of final cause and means: the operation will seem to run from the future as anticipated back to the past, and from the past forward to a future to be realized, and it will be this double-function which will stabilize past and future in a present as the most fundamental phase of this abstract medium. This present as ground and apex of past and future, is what makes "Permanence." Kant was right when he discovered the affinity of substance, time and permanence. But it is only for the reflective, the conceptual thought that past and future are substantially united in a present as permanent. There is no "permanence" in the pre-reflective extension of space-time, where the ground closes up against its articulation: it needs the building up of the ground by the accidental phases and it needs the stabilization of these phases, of past and future, in an expanded and thus permanent present. In this present, indeed, every step will be, as a step from the past, necessary, and as a step toward the future, possible, and vice-versa; it will be closed as well as open, just as concepts are closed and open on the road to truth. And these conceptual phases will be not so much "intuited," as "thought through," they will be as well particular as universal.

The stable present in which all phases are contained and balanced may be regarded as a "form," and thus another important structure of abstraction finds its place in the conceptual sphere. The final cause can be understood as a "Form." Although a distinction is usually made between the "final" and the "formal" cause, both are in fact only different aspects of the same device. Thus Aristotle indeed identified at times both, εἶδος and τέλος. The telos can be seen as a Form which has not yet realized its means; or the Form in its turn may be understood as a telos which stands in the accomplished balance of all its means. In the former case we may call the still unrealized means the "Matter" and distinguish it from its form. But as Plato rightly saw, matter can not be totally divorced from form, it is the means to the telos of form, and so Plato made matter "partake" **in form.**[8]

Form as a differentiated, conceptual entity, qualitative in its differentiation, gives at last also to the "whole" a new character: the whole was as a mathematical absoluteness, of a quantative character; but as a qualitative whole it has the nature of "completeness," of infinite completeness or "perfection." As such it has even entered the realm of theology as an attribute of God. But it is not more than a conceptual abstraction, a form which needs supplementation by Matter as the principle of incompleteness, of deficiency, relative to it. But the "complete form," as a lawful system is, indeed, the true fulfillment of the causal principle, is "causality thought through."

When we look back over the road which we have travelled, we find at the outset a unity of fact and order, characteristic for the realm of Logic. This unity splits up into number and method, figure and construction, and so Mathematics comes into its own. The breaking in of a mysterious Given, foreshadowed in the Infinite of the mathematical realm, welded operation and facts into the continuity of extension and gave, on the other hand, a factual independence to the elements of abstraction which, as substances, were involved in the paradox of causality and its operation. Reflection at last reconciled the paradoxes, uniting by concepts and laws the anticipation of meaning with an intention, never fully accomplished, until rest and fulfillment came into view through telos and form. But even the telos, the final cause, is only a step on the road to truth, every purpose turns out to be merely the means to a wider purpose, every form only the matter for a more advanced form. Therefore at the peak of the whole realm of abstraction a still higher unity is needed, a factuality which fulfills the universal outreach, a telos not divorced from its stages of realization, but contained in them as their integration, a form which cannot be abstracted from its matter, a substance which is one with its accidents and therefore neither substantial nor accidental, but beyond both. It is the idea of "Force," of "Power" which suggests itself at this point. Force has indeed entered the sphere of abstraction, even of

Science, with such inevitability that it has **had** to be adopted, although with reluctance and hesitation. A Newton who was skeptical with regard to laws as mere "hypotheses," had to surrender to the idea of Force and had to acknowledge "gravitational forces" as the ground of his laws. For "Force" is the ground of Law, is the "why" and necessity behind the law, the absolute and categorical fact above the hypothetical law-structure. Force is not a cause, for causes are facts "under the law," while forces are facts "above the law" as the absolute source of their necessity. Here, at the end of the route of abstraction, factuality rises again above intention, universality and order, as a Given of fundamental importance. Forces are not inferred as laws are, nor are they observed, as facts or instances, subordinated to law, are observed. Forces impose themselves on abstraction, though foreign to it, as messengers from another world. It is not the telos that is the link to reality beyond abstraction, and it is surely not the principle of life, as Kant thought: it is Force which assumes this role. Thus "Being" reveals itself here ultimately as Force or Power. But although this may be so and although "meaning" and "Truth" may be approached as Force or Power, symbolized by concepts and laws, abstraction is totally unable to cope with this ultimate reality, it can neither close it directly into its pattern nor understand it by its limited devices. The best, abstraction can do, is to characterize Force by its own irrational ground, the Infinite, and thus regard Force as "infinitely inexhaustible." Not "completeness" as derived from the absolute whole, but inexhaustibility is the characteristic of this Force. It is interesting to see that even the idea of "perfection" changed from completeness to inexhaustibility in the history of religious thought, in its application to the Divine.[9]

Science wavered among all modes of law, as form or as telos, before it tentatively adopted the idea of force. Science preferred the logical order of identity, strongly emphasized in its closed system and in the structure of its classifications. It adopted besides the mathematical method and introduced equality in mechanical causation, formulating its laws in mathematical terms, reducing its object to quantitative relations and measurable magnitudes. With Aristotle the emphasis had lain for a short time on telos and eidos, on a formative character of the universe, a doctrine mirrored to a certain degree in our modern theories of a curved space responsible for the behaviour of its content, and in the theories of physical fields and waves. The telos is also implicitly recognized in Hamilton's principle, in Planck's quantum-theory and in organic science. But, on the whole, the teleological interpretation has been regarded as a heresy, and replaced mostly by the other devices of abstraction, which seemed safer to the scientist. The advance into Force and Power, however, remains an adventure, highly distasteful and to be discarded as quickly as possible.

The idea of Force appears only dimly at the horizon of abstraction, never wholeheartedly accepted as legitimate. We will meet this idea of Force, however, in the concrete realm of reality, beyond abstraction. But it will always remain a mark of genius on the part of Aristotle that he discovered Force in the intentional dynamics of propositional abstraction as his "energeia," included in it the telos as "entelecheia," and even extended its outreach beyond abstraction into the realm of Being, where Force, more fundamental than law and necessity, discloses the reign of Freedom.

SECOND PART: REALITY

V. LIFE, WORLD AND EXISTENCE

Twice in the course of this work Reality appeared at the horizon, first as the Given, as the closed and indivisible continuum of space-time, rejecting and excluding the findings of abstraction, the things and their relations; then as "Being," as Truth, overarching and confirming the concepts which abstraction provided. In both cases this message from another world was accepted by abstraction from its own perspective and became thus a fundamental feature of abstract thought. Immanence is characteristic of abstraction, the dualism of transcendence is still undiscovered; wherever rationalism builds its abstract world, in Science or in a scientifically oriented philosophy, a balanced self sufficiency spreads over the monistic unity of the world. Neither failure nor evil nor the danger of doubt invades this realm, and thus it has always been one of the characteristic factors of rationalism, either to deny any status to evil and failure, or at least to regard them as mere accidental aberrations. There are dialectical tensions, to be sure, but they are lastly healed in the reconciliation which the conceptual stage provides, uniting in the form of a symbolic fulfillment process and phase, universal and particular, intention and realization. Even Truth does not really transcend this sphere, but fulfills itself in each of its symbols, and so it assumes the role of an absolute telos which confirms the stability and self-sufficiency of the abstract sphere and its immanence. The God of this realm is the Pantheistic Deity, immanent in its system of perfection.

This balance of immanence is broken, when Reality invades the sphere, and this invasion finds its fundamental expression in the searching and questioning process, in the "Eros" of Plato and the "Dynamis" of Aristotle. Into this questioning process Reality enters as a "problem." There are no problems in the abstract sphere, in the immanence of intention and fulfillment. There are tensions in the field of abstraction, but they carry with them their own healing power. But now Reality is "thrown in the way of" the process, as this is the literal meaning of the "Problema." Thus it is foreign to the process, entering from another world which is not included nor anticipated, as Truth was anticipated in its symbols. The cause was no problem for its effect, nor was the whole for its parts, nor the necessary for its possibles. They belong together in spite of a dialectic tension; they support each other mutually and provide a balanced security. It is the beauty of the abstract sphere that there is always ground under our feet, that answers are present even before any question has been asked, a system and totality of answers. This system of answers bounds the young life of the child, unquestionable, secure, enjoyed, lasting until the adolescent is suddenly faced with the "question"; then security goes to pieces, and the realization dawns that life is a struggle and a responsibility to be faced. In this problematic reality man grasps his own status and the loneliness of his questioning and doubting urge; threatened as he is by the sudden breaking in of another world, he becomes a problem to himself. Perplexity, astonishment, as Plato and Aristotle knew, are the signs attending the birth of philosophy; the emergence of the unfamiliar, the strange, raises to man the problem of himself. It is this problematic aspect of the questioning process which has hindered the attempts of philosophers to find a status for the Eros who seemed excluded from Reality as merely subjective, coming from nowhere. At the beginning of this work it was "abstraction" which seemed to break away from reality, and this primordial breach, the breach between fact and thought, was never fully overcome, in spite of the various solutions which abstraction offered. Here this breach opens even wider, as the breach between a questioning, doubting, searching drive and a reality which as the fulfillment of this drive is removed into a far-away distance. This distance is never bridged, although the questioning drive takes advantage of all the attempts of abstraction to heal the breach, closing in on answers which are not really answers but only signposts on a road which stretches into infinity. Fact and order, thing and its accidents, space-time and its places, the propositional process and its conceptual phases—all this balance and structure of abstraction is drawn into the current of a questioning drive, and now is subservient to this drive, articulating in answers the unending process, answers which are coined as symbols of abstraction but are again and again drawn back into the stream. The whole structure of abstraction now finds its true meaning, its setting and place in the searching drive and must be viewed in the light of this dynamic procedure. Thus the results of abstraction turn out to be no ultimate answers but rather further formulations of the problem in the form of answers, serving for future questioning. It is ultimately the question which survives in them and is carried forward step by step through them. Things and laws will still be possibles and necessities in the realm of truth; but in the face of the searching drive, in the current of this process, they are, even as necessities of truth, only possibles with regard to reality; and although they continue to play a role as possibles in the conceptual truth, they point as possibilities of a different kind to the realm of reality where no fulfillment awaits them. It was Aristotle who discovered beyond the abstractly possible and the abstractly necessary, the "Potential," which in spite of its necessity in the sphere of abstraction remains a possible with regard to reality. The Potential may seem independent in its symbolic necessity, but it is lost in spite of this independence, longing for reality and deprived of a reality which as a problem remains beyond its reach and renders the searching process, problematic with all its symbolic phases, a perpetual possibility. For it is this possibility, not the symbolic necessity which takes the lead in that which is called the "Potential."

We may pause here a moment in order to look back on the road we travelled and to throw some light ahead. Greek thought, as it was gathered up and lifted to a sublime consistency of system by Plato, was fully aware of the realm of abstraction, and its last and most urgent concern was the truth-value of judgment, of propositional thought. From here Aristotle took over, broke the crust of abstraction and discovered in the very process of propositional thought, in the "subjectum" of this process, an underlying reality which although never exhausted revealed itself in potential phases. These potential phases point now beyond abstraction as such and throw this abstraction into deficiency, into "privation" as a transitional and questionable stage. "Metaphysics" means from now on the insight into a higher realm, disclosed by the questionable structure of abstraction.

Thus abstraction itself has changed in the face of a reality beyond. Order, fact, substance, cause, concept and law are still valid, but they are dependent, subservient to a higher reality and they fall short of this reality. It would have been more adequate, perhaps, to present abstraction right from the start as involved in potential dynamism, made doubtful and undermined by a higher power. But we devoted the first part of this work to abstraction pure and independent, not only as an expedient procedure to get at each of its findings in its undisturbed clarity of structure, but also as the most congenial way to treat a realm which essentially omits, abstracts and puts itself on an independent footing. "Mind" as the vehicle of abstraction has in the history of thought repeatedly set itself up as an independent entity. Although its claim as such is unjustified, it points in its seeming independence to a wider spiritual center in which it is embedded: it points to the process of "personality" beyond abstraction and mere potentiality. But at present we are concerned only with the transitional aspect of the potential where abstract answers are put forth and taken back again into the process.

It is this process of questioning and doubting which is driven forward, nowhere to rest, nowhere to be fulfilled. It feeds on answers and may be regarded as necessary in these answers, but it destroys the answers and remains, in spite of being perpetually fed by them, hungry and dissatisfied. It is the problematic Reality, dimly appearing in a distance and looming unreachably over the process, which renders the process itself and all its achievements deficient. This reality is, of course, not "in relation" to the potential process and its phases, for relation is an abstract device and usable only between entities on the same level. The reality which is unrelated and absolute is, however, a power toward which all potentials are rising, although they vanish in the attempt without ever reaching or even anticipating this goal. The chain of potentials, cut off from absolute reality, is therefore itself unrelated, and can be called absolute in the sense of the accidental, expressing the abandonment which grips the potential process with its steppingstones of abstraction, detached from the real and thrown into the insecurity and twilight of a doubting and questioning drive. In vain abstraction may try to free itself from the power of reality and to set its own symbols up as the fulfillment of the process, raising conceptual fixities and necessary laws to idols which it worships as an eternal reality. It will only frustrate the searching process and stop the potential advance, losing sight of even that reality which clouded and dim, remained in a problematic distance. Aristotle, although the discoverer of the Potential, was not always free from this attitude, he too blurred the transitional character of the potential and gave it at times a pseudo-fulfillment in a conceptual "anticipation."[1] We may be allowed to use the language of such an anticipation, because concepts enter in and articulate the potential process: we should be aware, however, that these anticipations are restricted to the symbolic level of abstraction and do not carry with them any fulfillment of the questioning drive. When we call a baby a "potential child," the child a "potential adolescent," the adolescent a "potential adult," we should know that none of these conceptual anticipations fulfills the process. The process continues beyond them. Aristotle pointed to this truth when he characterized these way-stations, these answers embedded in the questioning process, as "longing" and "stretching out" beyond any fixety of a symbolic nature.[2] It is, as Aristotle saw, a "privation" which arrests the process, and therefore these privations are imbued with a longing and stretching out, perpetually undoing the arrest. Whenever we envisage an activity which obviously and unmistakenly carries beyond all way-stations, then and only then are we truly in the realm of the potential.

The prototype of such an activity is "Life." Life is an activity, the meaning of which is its unfolding in ever new possibilities, which never fulfill themselves in a result detachable from the process. For there can not be anything which might assume the role of a necessary goal for life as a directed and infinite process. Life remains a possibility, necessary only in this perpetual continuation. This potential process, transcending its symbolic anticipations, never realized in any of them but using them, feeding upon them, finds its clearest expression, when we consider it as a living "Consciousness." Consciousness is life which necessarily uses but surpasses a "content." There can be no consciousness without a content, and by so much consciousness is dependent on content. But there can also be no consciousness which does not pass beyond its content, unfulfilled by it, destroying it, absorbing it and perpetually restoring above it its own open and unfulfilled possibility.

The problem of consciousness and its content comes most clearly into focus, when we are faced with the problem of "the knower and the known." There is no such problem in the sphere of pure abstraction and its monistic immanence. It needs the dualism between process and content, the detachment of the process over against its content, to bring the problem of knower and known to the fore. In the propositional realm the process was subservient to its conceptual terms, the process even took here as a "subjectum" the humble place of a term at the side of another term, the subject besides the predicate, itself of a predicative nature, a symbol standing for the truth. But now, in the realm of potentiality, the process has detached itself from its predications and has risen above them. If we return once more to the realm of abstract thought, we are aware that here the process as it works in operation and in intention is always subjected to a factual fixety which ultimately rules over it, as is the case in "order," in "substance," and in "law." But in the potential realm the process is released by that distant power of reality which, confronting abstraction, raises the process above its content as a longing toward reality, a stretching out and striving for it, a potential procedure which uses and subjects the devices and operations of abstraction to its own forward drive. It may seem absurd that "Reality" is instrumental to the rising of process above abstraction and to detaching it from its facts. But this is exactly what lies behind the doubt and insecurity into which the process is thrown by a reality which has deprived it of its abstract defenses. As long as the process was subjected to its defenses, it received a pseudo-security from this subjection. But now, deprived of this security, the process is plunged into questioning and restless doubt, aware in this doubt of its own power, but at the same time aware of its weakness in the face of a high and unreachable reality.

We should therefore reserve the term "process" only for the potential drive which works in the continuity of a life-process, raised as consciousness over its content, and use the term "operation" or "function" for those subordinated, relational procedures which operate only between and in dependence upon abstract conceptual structures and therefore belong to these structures, that is, to the content of consciousness. Such operations as the causal function or the intentional operation in propositional thought are, seen from consciousness, embedded in the content, are discharged in the terms of the content, fulfilled in those terms, anticipating them, and thus belonging really to their inner structure. But the process of consciousness rises above this whole structure, including the operations, faces in its course a distant reality, and dismisses its content, with all its operations as unsatisfactory and inadequate. The difference, therefore, between the process and its operations or functions can not be stressed too strongly. It reflects clearly the transition from a realm, where abstract fixeties rule, to a realm where all these abstractions are reduced to mere contents of consciousness, subjected to the process. In this way the "knower" is born and the knowing process as distinct from the "known." This "known content" has its own articulation and operation, and thus, in spite of its subjection to the knower, it is detached from the knower. It is both "his known," embedded in the knowing consciousness, and at the same time it is "objectively known," an answer in its own right, always ready to set itself above the knowing process, and at times threatening to arrest this process. But here is no answer without the question which lives in it and drives beyond it, destroying the false self-sufficiency of the answer and taking it back into the process of questioning. The answer, as known, is known only in order to be transformed in the process of knowing, disappearing in the process, swallowed up by the process—a process which not only includes answers as known, but provides also the destructive outreach beyond any answer in the subjective attitude of the knower.

It can not be denied, of course, that the known in spite of its subjection to the knowing process is not concerned about the knower; it is in its turn apart, detached from the knower, and points to an intended truth which is by so much not affected by the subjectivity of the knower. Here the problem rises whether and how far this objective structure of truth is a door to that reality which in the distance looms over life and is "longed for" in the process of knowing. Rationalists have gone so far as to identify the objective structures of truth with reality as such. But the knower does not know reality in the way in which the thinker thinks truth, he knows only "about reality," using symbols of truth which never exhaustibly fulfill the longing for reality. In order to "know about reality" the knower will proceed over the abstract symbols and their operational structuring; they will be included but transcended in this knowing process which is indeed more complex, more problematic, and less stable than the mere "thinking of truth."[3] Knowing about reality perpetually destroys the symbolic answers and remains open and unfulfilled. Reality enters into this process mainly[4] by throwing the knower into the despair of his deficiency, making him doubt and question, so that here reality is responsible for the split in life, the split between consciousness and its stages, between the process and its content. We surely cherish life's infinite striving, never to be exhausted in any of its stages, as a noble aspiration, and to be alive is a glory scarcely to be surpassed; but, on the other hand, to be merely alive is contemptible: we want a content which in spite of being perpetually surpassed gives to our life some structure and stability. There is an element of uneasiness, of instability, of "chance," however, in the knowledge about reality, an element which has at times been confused with freedom. But the knower is not really "free" in his knowing, neither free nor totally determined. He is in an ambiguous and problematic status, caught between freedom and necessity, neither a creator of knowledge nor an automaton forced into the track of the known. Philosophers have wrestled with this unique character of knowledge; they have recognized the element of receptivity in the knower, and also the active "assent" which the knower has to give. But they have misinterpreted the latter as an act of free will. There is hesitation, choice and chance in the process of knowing, and doubt and question will keep the process perpetually open to error, so that the consciousness is involved in answers to which it assents, but which it also has to dismiss as unsatisfactory, and the assent as well as the dismissal are shadowed by chance, by uneasiness and by dissatisfaction.

Because of this twofold aspect of the known, rejected as well as confirmed by the process of life and consciousness, the process itself assumes a twofold character. On the one hand, it seems perpetually to end in answers which it is forced to destroy; on the other hand, it rises perpetually to ever new content which carries it continuously in its aspiration. If we concentrate on the first of these aspects, an objective series of fixed answers comes into focus, absorbing the questioning, the knowing process which thus seems lost in the structure of the known, becoming "unconscious" of itself and its direction the more the independent content stands out before the darkened ground of consciousness. What we here call the "Unconscious" is, however, not a blank nothing, an emptiness, a mere lack. It still retains the power of consciousness responsible for the formation of the conscious content, although it is dimmed down and seemingly lost in this content. The Unconscious is an element in, and related to, the conscious content; there is no sense attached to an "absolute Unconscious," just as there is no meaning in an absolute nought. The Unconscious is continually "made" unconscious, drowned in and by the conscious structure of content which as an objectivity eliminates the subjective source out of which it rose. We are here faced with a phenomenon similar to that which we met in the "absolute fact," raised out of and made absolute by a self-effacing thought. In consciousness, however, the Unconscious does not merely take its place at the side of the fact which it constitutes, as was done in the abstract realm: here the Unconscious remains a power, destroying what it helped to create, taking it back into the process, undermining it as it was itself undermined by the content which plunged it into Unconsciousness. In this way also the content itself becomes unconscious, dimmed down by a dynamic consciousness which rises, as we will see, perpetually out of its extinction in the content. Thus process and content build each other and destroy each other in unconsciousness,—in an unconsciousness of direction and in an unconsciousness of content,—and so they receive in this mutual interaction an unstable, a chance-character. Life seems to die in each of its experiences, whereby the experience of death is a dimmed-down-experience, an experience of the Unconscious, swallowed up again by the power of life; for life is strong enough, even in its darkened stage, to break the fetters of death only in order to die in always new experiences, so that living seems rather what Heraclitus called it, a perpetual dying. It is essential to the potential sphere that process and content undermine each other mutually, debasing life by death, consciousness by the Unconscious, and the reality of the known by an element of the Unreal.

We may at this point emphasize once more the distinction made above between an unconsciousness of direction and an unconsciousness of content, for this leads to the acknowledgement of a twofold consciousness too. Consciousness is aware of itself in its directedness, its continuity, passing over its content; and consciousness stands also in the limits of a content, arrested in this content. If the direction of consciousness is intensive, the content is dimmed down in this directedness; if the content as conscious is emphasized, the direction of consciousness is blurred. It is in this mutual dimming-down that the element of chance which we mentioned above finds entrance and becomes a characteristic feature of the relation of knower and known, misinterpreted, however, as a kind of freedom. There is indeed a "caesura," cutting process and content from each other, detaching the knower from the known and the known from the knower, a mutual estrangement effected by the unconscious. Thus both seem to be "freed" from each other, and this may have been the reason why thinkers have introduced freedom into the relation of the knower with the known. But consciousness and content are "freed" here only in order to lose themselves in hesitation, doubt and chance.

This chance-element which throws its shadow over the knowledge "about reality" conveys to the knower as well as to the known a character of unreality and unreliability. It is because of this that we regard the potential sphere of life, consciousness and its content, as "Appearance." The known, limited by a selection of content, apparently gathered accidentally out of the inexhaustible abundance of consciousness, and this consciousness apparently indefinite in its abundance and missing the clarity of the limited content, both deficient in the light of the other, disclose a diminished reality, and it is this which we call "Appearance."

Appearance thus expresses the antagonism between life and its content, both constituting and at the same time undermining each other and so leaving us in a state of uneasiness. It is not Reality as such which is responsible for what we call "appearance," and it is not this Reality itself "which appears." Appearance is a status of its own, manifesting the inner split in the potential sphere, the split between consciousness and content. From a higher perspective we may truly state that it is the dim awareness of a distant and problematic reality which throws life into its doubting and questioning drive, into arrest, unconsciousness and chance. But we are allowed to consider the potential sphere in its own structure and if we do this, then it is the schism in life itself which makes it to a mere appearance. The problem which has haunted philosophers since the time of the Brahmin thinkers: how reality can appear and how reality can lose itself in a sphere which is not fully real, but only apparent, is incorrectly put. It is life at the mercy of death, consciousness threatened by the unconscious that we experience as "appearance," as a status of its own and by no means a mere illusion or hallucination.

Life in its inner schism as appearance is, however, only one aspect of consciousness and its content: the other aspect, more important and more representative for the potential sphere, is the perpetual healing of this schism, is the ever rising power of life, rising above and surpassing its content, not as destructive merely with regard to this content, but carrying the content to a richer integration. Here consciousness, in the definiteness of its direction, is not vague and indefinite but inexhaustible, and it serves in this its inexhaustibility the content which it unfolds and to which it conveys the necessity of this unfolding, eclipsing the chance-element residing in the limited selection when arrested. Here life shows itself not as perpetually dying, but as an ever new birth.

Newness is an essential character of life seen in this light, for life perpetually sacrifices the old for the sake of the new. There is, of course, an inevitable "aging" in the process of experience, a shadow of death falling upon the knower, and nobody who is not aloof from experience can avoid aging through the impact of his experiences. But besides aging there is "maturing" which emphasizes not a loss but a gain, a growing richness. This growing richness is felt when we speak of life not as perpetually running out, losing, slipping away, but as a continuous enrichment, a creative renewal, and we may call life under this aspect: "imaginative." Imagination expresses life's unreality not less than appearance does, but this unreality is here caused not so much by an inner breach as by the transitoriness of the "images," by the ever new birth of content. The single image, therefore, when isolated and lifted out of its process, seems unstable, a mere expression of the infinite abundance of the imaginative process, unsharp in its contour and thus unlike the abstract answer. And unlike this conceptually stable answer the image yields readily to other and always other images. While the fixation of an abstract content holds out stubbornly in causes and effects, means and purposes, in things and substances, dying hard and leaving the scene only reluctantly, lingering on the threshold of consciousness as an "appearance,"—imagination as an urge for the ever new rushes ahead and happily acknowledges in each image the possibility of the next. Thus the image may not be as clearly delimited as the conceptual entity was, but it serves the directedness of consciousness in its dynamic unfolding. The fixed answer, as merely apparent, and destroyed in doubt and question, was "neither this nor that," but the image expresses an "as well this as that," reaching potentially beyond itself, satisfying in ever new images the unfolding direction and growing on its way.

Imagination has been handed over to psychology and explained as "sensation." But a phenomenon is not philosophically understood when derived from a body-function. Such a derivation, important for Natural Science, does not open any door to Metaphysics. Conceptual thought can not satisfactorily be explained by the brain, and imagination can not be elucidated by referring to eyes and ears. It is true that the processual flow of the imaginative content seems to weld with the equally processual character of consciousness and thus to assume in its turn a subjective character, as if the flow of images took place merely in the awareness of the knower and had no counterpart beyond this awareness, subjective only and in so far "irreal." But here it has to be emphasized, that imagination achieves an objectivity of its own and of a very different kind, more powerful and more immediate than the ever broken series of appearances which—in the conflict of consciouness and content and in their mutual extinction by the Unconscious—assume, in spite of their independence, a merely accidental character.[5] In the continuous flow of imagination both consciousness and content participating in the dynamism of a processual unity, unbroken and unweakened by conflict and not rendered accidental, proceed in a **necessary** advance which carries consciousness, intensified in unfolding and direction, forward toward an unknown objective power,— that very power which had freed process from its abstract structures. Thus consciousness is here lured on, devotedly and receptive, drawn by its imaginative content beyond itself into a submission, shaped more than shaping, in an attitude which we call "perceptive." Perception as an intensive awareness of a content which is necessitated in its unfolding, leads on and transcends beyond itself in its ever limited perspective of a subjective imagery. It knows, therefore, that its objective is never exhaustively grasped by its images and that the richness and many-sidedness of its object adumbrates the lighted realm of consciousness. Consciousness is here, therefore, in contrast to its apparent knowledge, not so much separated from its content,—the knower from the known,— but, in union with its content, separated, however from an unknown and totally independent object, toward which its imaginative drive is directed, deficiently grasping this object, in one perspective only besides other perspectives, and converging with these infinite other perspectives toward one and the same perceived "Nature" which opens up in the flux.[7] It has, however, to be emphasized that this dynamic necessity of the imaginative flow is only one of the two aspects of potential experience and that this aspect is never to be had without its counterpart of a reflective and merely apparent structure, never without submitting also to the partial drowning in the Unconscious and its static articulation. In this way accidentality is mixed to the necessity in one and the same inseparable experience which is imagination and reflection at once.

The manner in which the processual content of imagination is known is, however, very different from the way by which the abstract structure was conceived. The process of imagination is "felt" or "intuited"; the processual structure in its objectivity and abstraction is "thought." But, whether felt or thought, both ways of awareness are of a universally valid knowledge and of a more than subjective character. The intuited knowledge of the processual flow is concrete, not abstract, and its universality is grounded in its infinite outreach not in a finite intention of law. Thus the total knowledge of a living consciousness, felt and thought, will rely on the fixed phases of a content, but it will embed these phases in a dynamic process of imagery, in which every single entity loses itself in a passing flow and thus becomes "absent" in a past, captured, however, in an ever present and continuous stream of memory, blurred but compensated for its loss of clarity and distinctness by the richness of various shades, acquired in the merging and welding together of past images as well as from tendencies toward the future, into which it reaches in the process of its unfolding.

We are inclined to overemphasize the realism of the statically known, the sequence of fixed and abstract entities and the equally fixed relation in which they stand. But we should never omit the flux of processual imagination dominant in the known and rich in its variety. If we restrict ourselves to a scientific view, the static structure may suffice; but even here imagination will break in, for it is always somehow at work in our knowledge, supplementing the abstractly fixed answers and adding to the exact but empoverished content some of the richness which an abstract realism missed. In the realm of life an object is never merely what it appears to be in the static fixation of a rigid present: it comes from somewhere and it goes somewhere, and so it reaches into the distant regions where imagination provides its shades and colors. And when we approach the highest sphere of human knowledge in Religion and in Art, we will see that a static and abstract knowledge of a fixed present is wisely avoided: Religion will forbid any fixed presentation with regard to the object of its veneration, although it will allow it to be expressed in a narration; and Art will transform the abstract fixity of the known by the mysterious device of "stylization," again an imaginative richness of a processual variety.

It is the process of appearance and imagination, structured in fixed percepts, but surpassing them in an imaginative unfolding, "thought" extensively in its phases, and at the same time "felt" intensively in its direction and processual flow, articulated but continuous, objective, however, in all of its aspects, which we may now at last call by its name: it is the "perceptual space-time" or the "process of a living Duration."

This lived process of duration, objective in flux and articulation, is certainly no order and certainly not identical with abstract space-time, discussed in a former chapter. It is objectively "given" to things and events, and in so far it resembles, indeed, the ground of abstract space-time. But while the given ground of abstract space-time conveyed duration only to things and remained itself in the background untouched by this duration, the living process of duration is itself essentially enduring, in a conscious integration of the present, conveyed to it by its directedness to the eternally enduring reality. But it is also aware of its ever changing character, sharing the varying aspects of its content and thus at the same time enduring in this very change. It is the processual character of the consciousness as well as of the flow of content which unites both to such a degree, that they —process of consciousness and process of content—have often been erroneously identified, participating both in one and the same pattern of duration.

It is this complex nature of a process,—intensive as well as extensive, subjective as well as objective, working in us and at the same time conditioned by an independent reality, —which we grasp in the phenomenon of **"motion."** Motion is a process of duration, constituted by the process of consciousness and its direction, but constituted also by the content in its flow, by the objective flux of images which presents itself to our consciousness. This complex character of Motion, subjective and objective, intensive and extensive, enduring and changing, has involved in unsolvable problems. Even the ingenious analysis, which Aristotle offered, did not do full justice to this complexity, but reduced it to a sequence of phases, emphasizing rather the abstract appearances in their discontinuous series, while the continuity of the process was supplemented by a lose "operation" between these phases, every phase reaching out from its fixity to the next, building thus the process out of constituting pieces of non-motion.[8] But motion is, in fact not constructed out of phases, it is an indivisible unity of process, which—although fed by ever changing aspects of content—perpetually transcends this content and makes it disappear in the dynamism of its flow. Natural Science, however, could use this Aristotelian reduction into a sequence of phases, exemplified by an object, carried in the flux and elucidating the sequence by the change of its positions in the process. But life and philosophy are in need of an insight which keeps the "passage" of motion intact, the indivisibility of the flux.

There is, of course, "articulation" in the indivisible process of motion, because of the reflective element, resulting from abstract appearances, but this reflective element of articulation has to be grasped in a way which discloses not only the articulating aspect but also its absorption in the process, its vanishing in the dynamism. We may call it the "momentum" in the motion. This momentum is a kind of "here-now," but it is an intensive integration of directedness, very different from the "here-now" we discussed in the realm of abstract space-time. The dynamic and intensive momentum contains past and future, but the past is here not just a phase of "before" and the future not just a phase of "after," the latter anticipated and reflectively carried out in steps of the past, whereby each step is outside of the other in extension. The "momentum" of motion is the intensive center of the present, from which past and future radiate; they too are intensities and will diminish in as much as they depart from the present as the source of their intensity. Abstraction will interpret this departure as an extensive distance and will because of the mutual exclusion of phases in extension place the past outside of the present as being "not anymore," and the future equally outside as being "not yet." In this way objects in their transition from present to past will seem to lose themselves in absence, although intensively they remain present, and it is this presence which consciousness will realize by memory and expectation. It is through memory and expectation that passing events can be grasped not only in their bodily presence, but also in that intensive presence which encloses past and future in the integration and flow of images, conveying to the events an abundance of varying shades, absent from the point of view of a bodily extended fixation. Thus memory and expectation are aspects of an intensive consciousness, objectively participating in the imaginative flow of an enduring content, radiating into the past and future by the abundance of their outreach as a widened present and enriching consciousness.

The momentum is, therefore, as well an element of consciousness, enriched by memory and expectation, as also an element in the processual content and objective flux. But even in its objective character the momentum is never static, neither as a here-now, nor as a thing. Things are extended here-nows and of interest in the process of motion only in so far as they manifest the changing of phases, important for measurement.

If we want to introduce here the category of "Substance," then we should rather regard the processual flow itself as "substantial," while the things as means of articulation have an "accidental" character, limited to the role of structuring the changing phases in the process, derivative with regard to this process. Consciousness will consider these things as informative with regard to the process in which they are embedded and will invent them for the sake of such information, if they are not observable, as Physics has amply done. Thus motion can not be regarded as **originating** in a thing, it merely uses the thing for its own articulation. But, indeed, it **has** to use things and a reflective articulation, it is tied to things inevitably. Things, although buried in the function and thus derivative from the function, are because of their indispensibility also necessary for the function. The role of mere possibility in the function and the role of necessity for the function alternate and give rise to a paradoxical unity of opposite insights. This paradox of opposing insights can best be understood, when we think of a very specific thing, the human body. The body is, on the one hand, absorbed and dissolved in a function which, although the function of a body, does not bring this body and its organs to the fore: We do not see the bodily organs of our eyes, but colors; we do not hear the receptive organ of our ear, but a stream of sounds. The body as a thing has cancelled itself for the sake of the function which, therefore, seems independent from the body, centered in the function of consciousness, a body-function, to be sure, but unconscious of the body. This consciousness carries on in a flow of images, or rather in a dynamism of images and sounds, and this dynamism assumes susbtantial character, a dynamic experience over and against the merely accidental and possible external body, the thing or static object. But, on the other hand, consciousness and dynamic function are just as much absorbed in and made accidental with regard to the body as a thing which in its turn assumes substantial nature, a necessity for the merely possible conscious-functions and dynamic processes of seeing, hearing, touching etc. This ambivalence of body and function separates both from each other, in making now the one, now the other into a mere accidentality which could also be not, and so the one and the other assume independence, a striking example and confirmation of that which we have explained about the Unconscious and its liberating power, liberating process from thing and thing from process.[9] But, in spite of this separation and abolishment of the one in the other, there is a unity between them, an inevitable reliance upon each other: Consciousness needs its fixed content, function needs its body; but, on the other hand, body needs also its functions, although it closes them into its substantial fixity, and both, body and function, are possible and necessary respectively and with regard to each other. Therefore an accidental atmosphere envelops here, in the sphere of sensation, the process as well as its achievements, although there is "necessity" present too and fools us by popping up now in the body, now in the function. This ambivalence—to make the paradox still more striking—is restricted not just to the specific thing, the "body," but characterizes, similar to the human body, all things, all objects which appear as well as fixed substantial entities as also reveal their nature as carriers of functions, as indicators of motion throughout the environment. It is this latter function, as carriers of motion, which is most representative for the perceptive grasp of what we call "Nature." Nature is, as we mentioned above, an independent and absolute reality toward which our bodily functions are directed, not affected by accidental subjective perspectives and never exhaustibly disclosed by our sensations. We will have to return to this problem later.[10]

That things "are," to a large degree, what they "do," is an insight, not to be dismissed lightly, and it has been adopted by modern Physics. Physics reduces its objects, whether observed or invented, to mere indicators of the motional process in which they are involved, and in which they manifest the direction of the unfolding, expressing not so much their own nature, as the "career" in which they are proceeding, "indefinite," "indeterminate" with regard to their isolated status, but definite and determined as to the direction of their career. Physical science, in as much as it keeps free from pragmatism and does not adopt the philosophy of positivism, avoids the onesided emphasis on subjective usefulness and the arbitrary surrender to man's needs; it is convinced of the importance and objectivity of a transcending process, necessary and independent in its direction, although accidental with regard to the indicators of this process, the things, which, arrested and isolated in their fixity, are not observable in definite form and blurred as to their definite "causal" relation to each other. The element of "chance" [11] which we met as affecting the relation of knower and known, and which the body reflected in its unconscious absorption, this element of chance affects also the scientific organization of knowledge. Seen from the perspective of the fixed objects or chance-phases and their relation to each other the necessity of the process, which is undeniable in its directedness, appears as an "accidental necessity," or, as we call it, a "probability." In this probable unfolding which is a unity of chance and necessity, chance-phases evolve in the direction of a necessary process and disclose a necessary law which stretches over the accidental phases as a "law of probability." Such a law of probability is not just a preparatory law, limited by our subjective ignorance and developing through better knowledge to the full rigidity of mechanical necessity; it is not just a "probable law." It is the ultimate statement of necessity which the potential sphere admits, it is the only kind of law possible in this realm and as such it does full justice to the structure of an object which is predominantly in motion and unfolding in potential phases. Therefore not only the Science of a nature in motion but also life as a potential process can only be evaluated in its probable necessity. Life's career is probable and never ascends to a stronger form of necessity, as far as it is just a vitalistic procedure. We may throw out before us into the course of our future career an anticipated necessity, the conceptual fixation of a purpose, in order to give to life an unrestricted necessity and security. But even then, even under the impact of the most elevated form of abstract necessity, life will remain only probable: it will subject the purpose, as it subjects all fixations in its course, to its own probable necessity, it will modify the purpose, introduce chance and so correct the anticipated and seemingly dominating necessity in the course of its realization. Life's unfolding is, even under the stress of a telos, a probable course, uncertain in every phase and received in anxiety and hope. If any life were to appear as necessary in the sense of Newtonian Physics, we would rightly be astonished and regard this as "improbable." It is just as improbable that a life should disclose a rigid necessity of causation without any open chances, than that a life should be nothing but a conglomeration of accidents. Sciences of life, such as Sociology, present therefore not laws of mechanical necessity but only laws of probability, as statements of a necessity indicated by facts, which, though individually indeterminate and colored by chance, disclose, when gathered up and grouped together, a necessity of direction in which deviations have cancelled each other, producing an "average" of statistical lawfulness.[12]

The insecurity of life's probable course has shocked and frightened man. It has made him withdraw at times into the secure haven of an abstract structure. He has hypostatized the findings of exact thought and has taken refuge in things, substances, and causes. He has relied on laws, on fixed purposes and anticipations and has worshipped necessity as Science presents it. He has dismissed appearance and imagination from his mind, both as equally unreliable, exaggerating their deficiency as if they were dreams of confusion which blur the clear structure of a timeless order. Change and motion became symptoms of a disorderly "matter," and life itself either a phenomenon fitting no-where and being neither real nor dream, or a part of illusory confusion from which only death can liberate.

This escape from life could not remain merely a detached and disinterested claim for truth, it took on religious fervor and entered the Christian creed, where it enveloped life with darkness and gloom. Eastern Christianity, more than the Christianity of the West, regarded this life as hopelessly forlorn, without any meaning or value, to be patiently born until death brings release. Philosophy can not follow this road, it must restore life's truth in spite of deficiency and mere probability. Philosophy has to recognize the different layers involved in the potential sphere, it has to understand the complexity of the perceptual duration which uses the devices of abstraction, uses things, substances, causes, builds them into the structure of law, but makes reflection lastly subservient to its own course, proceeding over all these entities in its infinite and inexhaustible motion, not hostile, however, to them and not really endangered by their fixity, but fostered on its way by the articulation which they provide. Thus philosophy has to do justice to the complexity of appearance and imagination, fixation and flux, extensive sequence and intensive radiation, a complexity to which memory and expectation amply contribute. For memory and expectation not only reach into past and future, as mentioned above, radiating intensively from a present center into past and future. They are at work also with regard to the extended phases of past and future, separated from each other, the one as not any more, the other as not yet. Here memory and expectation have by a specific effort to bring past and future into the present, here memory has to "recall" the past, and expectation has to "anticipate" the future in order to lodge the events which are gone and those which are to come in the present. The present, which in this way assumes a widely extended volume, not only stores the events of the past but also allows them to circumscribe a horizon for future events to come. And our anticipation of the future, on the other hand, will select and limit the events, worth recalling. Thus the present becomes a meeting-ground for past and future, on which past and future clash in narrowing each other's scope and power. The past will eat itself into the future and will by limiting its horizon subject the future to its own pattern, as if the future were nothing but the realization of the past. The future, similarly, will seem to absorb the past for the sake of its own growth, feeding on it to nourish its insatiability. It will, indeed, be the present in which this battle is fought, but the bitterness of the fight will be softened by the quietness and stability of the intensive duration with its radiation into past and future. In so far memory and expectation will integrate past and future in a peaceful way: the past will be united with the present as "still" alive and the future will be similarly united in the present as "already" alive, and so both, participating in the present will add to each other's strength which is the strength of the radiating power of the present. There will be no mutual weakening, but a mutual enriching.

Mythology and Poetry have emphasized now the one and now the other of these contrasting attitudes. The sad truth was proclaimed that Time devours its children and finally results in Nought, life being a "tale told by an idiot," a making and unmaking in alternation, like the web of Penelope. Melancholic poets pointed to the wisdom that there is nothing New under the sun, and that what seemed a future was only the repetition of the past. But then again enthusiasts and religious visionaries hailed life as a perpetual birth and discovered that age and death do not really affect the values of this world, that there is a perpetual renewal, that all wounds are healed by time, and that life is a glorious adventure.

Pessimism and Optimism color these mythological and poetical perspectives which capture only one aspect of life and discard the other. There is undoubtedly truth in both of these views and the attitudes which they inspire. They are both concerned with an integration of life's opposing elements, its flow and its closed phases, and they ground themselves either in the extensive present in which the phases seem to destroy each other or in the intensive momentum of direction through which the present becomes a center of growth and enrichment. Thus past and future indeed destroy or build each other up, according to the point of view taken and according to the parts which past and future are allowed to play. But the philosopher has to see beyond these parts, he has to grasp the full life with its different aspects and roles to play; he has to know that loss is united with gain, creation with destruction, and that the full integration of life finds its expression in the balance of contradicting tendencies. He is aware of the tension of opposites, a tension which comes into focus in a feeling, a "mood." Mood is a feeling born out of a tension which thought can not resolve. Mood is fed by loss and gain, it is the realization and awareness of passing away and of coming to be, of death and of birth. It combines the sadness of loss with the sweetness of memories, the joy of gain with the bitterness of its futility. Mood as a modality of consciousness is a tension, a restlessness, a lack of stability, but on the other hand, feelings and moods protect against the complacence of fixed results and the laziness of going to rest. "Mood" is a more adequate term than "feeling," for the latter has been used in too many senses. Mood as a tension is in every awareness of life's duration. It gives a certain character to our experience, even a kind of insight, and is at times more decisive than any fixed reflection standing out before our consciousness.

But the mood is not constituted only by the ups and downs, by differences of our experiences, it is also dependent on what we may call the "tempo" of the changing phases. Tempo is generally thought of as a quantitative relation, and this is surely one of its aspects, but tempo is qualitative as well. Tempo is an outstanding example of the unity of the abstract and concrete, and therefore well fitting into the transitional realm of life; it is thought as a quantity and felt as a quality, as a mood. We may measure a tempo and fix a number to it, but more important in our context is the mood that different tempi carry. There is a tension in tempo, a holding back and a driving forward. This is obvious when tempi vary and when in the contrast with each other the one appears as retarding, the other as pushing ahead, the one lingering as if reluctant to leave, the other hastening as if leaping toward the future and fleeing from the past. But even in cases where no change in tempo occurs, not slow and quick in alternation, but where only one flowing tempo preserves its character, equal in its course, the articulating phases are in a tension of a mutual interaction, each phase somehow held back in the past, retarded and arrested in its fixity as if slowed down by its own weight, but at the same time drawn forward, lured by the future and stretching out into it, leaping in quickened motion toward its successor. The double aspect of separation and unification, which Aristotle detected in the "now" of the time-process, is here a dynamic tension of potentials, holding back and driving forward in every moment of the tempo, and making this moment tremble in the tension of the process. The articulating moments are not static entities, merely added one to the other, they are potentials of the tempo and express it in their own dynamic tension.

Mood and tempo characterize the potential process. Life, consciousness, duration will always be colored by mood and tempo. Young people will rush forward into the future and hasten in a quick tempo through the past which serves them only as material for the ever attracting future, always ahead of themselves. Old people, on the other hand, will linger in the past and hesitantly and slowly let the past lead into the future, which will be felt merely as the means for the growing treasure of the past. But not only do the young and the old have different tempi and moods, so do races and historical periods. One need only compare medieval with modern man to see how life may take on different tempi and different moods.

Tempo and mood belong, however, only to the sphere of life and duration, to the deficient sphere of appearance and imagination. When we reach into the depth of ethic, art, and religion, neither tempo nor mood will be an essential characteristic. They may still play some small role in these spheres, but they will color only the surface. They will be replaced by the more profound dynamism of "Rhythm" and by such feelings which are more intensive than mood ever can be. To regard tempo and mood as essential—for instance in Art—would be a grave mistake committed by a psychological vitalism.

So far we have treated the potential sphere entirely on its own account and we have seen it confirming itself in the loss and gain of its phases. The sphere of a full realization of the potential, of "actuality" beyond appearance, has not found an adequate manifestation, although we could not deny that the potential was perpetually rising toward a higher realm. The dualism of levels was also dimly apprehended in the endeavor of the knower to raise his knowledge to an independent status, but this endeavor remained unfulfilled and was finally defeated in the apparent and imaginative knowledge. For even imagination failed to bring reality into focus, as much as it was driven by a higher power. It is now the time to correct and to supplement the predominantly immanent view to which the potential sphere still clings as its most characteristic attitude. We are indeed inclined to be satisfied with an apparent life of imaginative knowledge, and it is only in rare moments that this attitude is broken by an aspiration which, dissatisfied with the merely potential process and its selfconfirmation, reaches out to another sphere, although an abyss may separate this aspiration from its objective. Disturbed by a restlessness, created by a life of moods, tempo, imagination and appearance, this aspiration will seek a reality beyond the kind of objectivity which images, symbols and apparent answers provide, always undermined by doubt. It will seek a reality which as unquestionable may stand out beyond the grasp of life's imaginative process. This seeking will be "felt," but this feeling will pierce beneath the surface where mood can spread. It will be more disruptive and dangerous, more dynamic and revolutionary than mood, but also more devoted and guided by its objective. We call such a feeling "Emotion." Emotion should be clearly distinguished from mood. While mood plays with possibilities, with loss and gain, stable only in the tension of its ambivalence, Emotion has a firm direction in its dependence on its objective which is not lost and gained, nor maintained in the alternation of ups and downs, confirmed lastly only in this play of phases: It is rather that the whole of life is offered as a loss to something more than life, something which deserves to be gained. There is a certain violence in emotion, a lack of balance, for there is more at stake than balance. The future now overpowers the past, and the forward-drive assumes an intensity not known before, forcing the past into the mould of the future. What we call "irreversibility" of direction comes here into focus. There was direction already in the operation of abstraction and in the structuring of abstract space-time, and, of course, there was direction in the lived duration. But the irreversibility of direction is quite another matter, and it is forced into life by the overpowering character of the future, as the objective of an emotional drive. Neither duration as a balanced present nor the mood which goes with it and feeds on the mutual interaction of past with future, on loss and gain, has this irreversibility.[13] It needs the breaking in of the future, destroying irretrievably the past, tearing open an abyss, forcing us to break the bridges behind us and to lance ourselves forward toward our objective. Only when the balance is changed in favor of the future, has the full impact of life's irreversible drive come into existence. The future which in this way breaks into life is not life's own making but ingresses from another sphere, and it is here, and here only, that this other sphere openly enters the potential realm. The biological immanence and monism of Bergson's earlier writings has made him miss this future, so that his "élan vital" seems to evolve only from past to present. What influenced Bergson here was, besides his emphasis on immanence, the identification of future with the intentional anticipation of a purpose, which as an abstraction he rejected. But the future which breaks in from beyond is not an abstract anticipation: what we anticipate are events in the future, not future as a power, just as we recall only events of the past, not the past as such which forms itself in the working of the future. Future and past, in the sense in which they are faced here, are known by emotion and are known in the intensive and irreversible direction which only emotion provides.

Here the subjective pragmatic view of the potential imagination, of environment and body, finds its correction under the impact of a Given, a Reality beyond. In spite of its subjective aspiration and its submerging of body and environment in the consciousness of the knower, imagination reaches out beyond body and things—not back to the subject as pragmatism wants us to believe chaining us to the inbred life of vitalism—, but to something not sensed, not structured by the body and its organs. That the sense-world is not altogether exhaustively explained by a subjective psychology, was mentioned above: it is the bridge between the subject and a reality of at least equal power, a reality "about which" imagination could discern only fragmentary facets and which, therefore, seemed to be subjected to a pragmatic concern. Pragmatism was right in reducing the sense-structure to tools, means, organs, bridges, suggesting something else beyond, but it was wrong in stopping short at the subjective consciousness and allowing these tools, means and bridges to lead back again to the subject and its arbitrary needs. It is the emotional striving for an Objective beyond the sense-realm [14] which gives to this very sense-realm an objectivity, imagination itself is not able to reach, although it tends toward it and is adumbrated by it, so that the distortions of a local body-perspective are corrected and we are allowed to claim a universal knowledge of "Nature," valid for everybody. This is so, because consciousness transcends its merely subjective seclusion and, directed to an objective beyond, renounces the useful mastering of things into possessions, humbly concentrated upon a reality as its objective which can not be possessed, but which remains over against the aspiration of the knowing consciousness. The "Nature" which in this way presents itself to the emotion as its objective is, therefore, not a "thing" and not an image. This Nature, striven for in aspiration, will in this aspiration be felt as "responding," for response is the quality which opens up to the emotional outreach. What we fear or hope, what fills us with enthusiasm or terror, is not so much a neutral object, fixed in its boundaries, reliable and predictable in its abstraction: it is rather an indefinite power, as it has indeed been vaguely divined in primitve religions, residing either in things or beyond things, and unlike, in its working, to mere abstract causality, it was linked to "life," but as a sinister and hostile power of life, responding more by threat than by inspiring confidence. In whatever way, however, this Nature may respond, it is regarded as a living power, and so it is understandable that from time immemorial not only religious thinkers, but also the great metaphysicians imbued Nature with life, from Greek Hylozoism on to Plato and Aristotle, further to Spinoza and Leibnitz, and in our own time to Bergson and Whitehead, Rationalism, of course, had to purify Nature for its purposes from any element of an emotional kind, in order to close it in the firm framework of its abstract laws. Emotion was rightly regarded as the source of insecurity and unbalance, and thus the foreground-structure of fixed things and their relation was freed from the emotional ground which Metaphysics could not discard. The question arises, however, whether a world, sterilized from emotion, is still real or whether it is a dream only, and whether man, protected by this dream, has not lost contact with true reality.

The reality to which emotion aspires as its objective and which responds to the aspiration is a future which never becomes a past: it is rather to be regarded as a present, overarching the imaginative sequence of pasts and futures. In the face of this unchanging, always present future the duration of consciousness and the processual content of an objective motion receive the ultimate character of "passage," of a passing flow. At the beginning of this chapter we saw that the process of consciousness rose beyond the structure of its static content, because it was released by a power, by a reality not included in its drive; and we recognized furthermore that, in being released, consciousness was not left to its own freedom, but was subjected together with its content, which now assumed a processual character too, to the strange power which had released it, sent on its way in doubt and questioning. These insights find here their confirmation. The passage, the flowing instability of duration, of any motion, is conditioned by the fateful power of a present, and it is the unchanging ground of this present, before which the passage runs its course and which gives to motion the nature of lostness, of "distentio" as St. Augustine calls it,[15] but also of being supported in its irreversible directedness, disclosed in its passage by the austere ground. Motion is relative, to be sure, but not only with regard to other motions; it is relative most of all to an absolute and unchanging ground. Science could not cope with the "passage" of motion, because its methods did not allow it to reach to the ground as the standard of absoluteness. Bergson's criticism of the denaturalized scientific concept of motion is correct. Science can not face this passage of motion, but the "scientist" as a living being, is, in spite of his elimination of the passage from the content of his inquiry, exposed to it: **he** will in doubt and anxiety feel the slipping away and losing of answers in the flux, but, at the same time, he will be confirmed in his aspiration to a truth beyond all his answers, convinced by his faith as to the absolute unity of the real. The scientist, not less than the common man, will feel emotionally directed to nature, which responds and has a "physiognomy" of its own for those who, exposed to the vicissitudes of life and close to nature, can not possibly reject the essential support which aspiration gives to the awareness of reality. In as much as we are unable to enter into the spiritual reality of ethics, art and religion without the emotional drive, so also the reality of Nature is closed, if the aspiration to the ultimate objective does not carry us beyond our petty needs and the usefulness of things.

It is, therefore, that we have to find a specific name for this Nature, a name which separates it from the foreground-perspective by which abstraction structures things. Such a name should not be quite unfamiliar, but it should, on the other hand, protect against confusion with the sphere of practical usefulness. When we consider the things around us in their usefulness and order them for our purposes into a fixed system, we speak of an "environment." But life is not totally fenced in by such an environment, it breaks at times through its fences and recognizes beyond the environment a "World." It is "World" which is sought for in our aspiration and is its objective.

Consciousness knows itself as over against the World and it receives in this confrontation with the World its full meaning. The first profound problem of man was formulated by the Brahmins: "Who am I in relation to the

World?" This World, received in aspiration, was deified and worshipped as God Brahma. But even when not deified, the World plays a decisive role in the life and development of man. When the environment with its fixed laws, customs, things, dogmas breaks, which tribe, family or church have erected around the youth, then the "initiation," the "conversion" sets in and "World" is discovered, a World, for which the emerging individuality feels responsible, for he has to make his way in this World.

The World is not a fact, and the consciousness faced by the World is not a thought process which extinguishes itself for the sake of the fact. Rather is the World an infinite process itself, before which the finite ego vanishes with all its symbols and structures. What positivism claims from its totally different point of view, that the systems of thought are only subjective structures, dictated by the limitations of our minds, may receive in the face of the World some semblance of truth. The selection which our observations make and which supports our findings, is very limited and, seen from the inexhaustible infinity of the World, rather arbitrary. In a "closed system"—and this is all we can observe—the possibilities which our observation is able to gather will soon be exhausted, processes will seem to come to a standstill, energies will disintegrate, without a resistance, and "entropy" will finally rule. But as much as science will need the closed system, the World is not such a system: here the possibilities are inexhaustible, every environment is kept going by its interaction with always new environments, and new forces coming into play. Entropy will be a bad dream, a manifestation only of the limited nature of our knowledge and the unreachable distance of a World which always remains a problem for man. But as much as man is separated from this World, it is nevertheless his World, given to him in his confidence. In his devotional emotion World is "given." The "Given" which as the mathematical Infinite, then as the ground of substance, of cause, of space-time and further as meaning, truth and Being stood behind our conceptual thought, all this is here "given" as the reality of World or Nature in a unity of aspiration and response. It is true that this Giveness can not be clothed into symbols and laws, although symbols and laws prepared for it. It is given in the confidence which, in spite of the insecurity of our futile life and the fear which it causes, brings us into the presence of the World. Man is not "thrown into the World" as Heidegger stated, adopting gnostic terminology. We live this World in anxiety, but also in hope, and in confidence. The World rises, stable as a rock, beyond the insecurity of our frail and fleeting life, not thought and not imagined, but somehow "suggested" by our experience. The pessimism of modern existentialism is a one-sided emphasis, caused by the impotence of a longing which knows reality as unreachable. But also the radical rationalist, not less than the existentialist, misjudges the World, turns away from it in order to find security in symbols which he hypostatizes, lifts a World of Ideas above the flux of life and worships it as his reality. The mediaeval thinkers had a profounder insight than their rationalistic ancestors, for they recognized beyond the sphere of mere "essences" a reality which they called in contradistinction to these essences "Existence."

The World is the Existence which is given to life and consciousness, but beyond its scope, untouched by the ever repeated beginnings and endings of our fleeting experiences. Life recognizes, however, its own unbalancedness in the face of this Existence and knows itself as a Naught, rejected in its subjectivity, rejected and at the same time called to receive Existence and to open toward its power. The Naught of our life may remind us once more of that Naught which as a self-extinction of thought was responsible for the absolute fact. But the Naught which is experienced in the presence of Existence does not take its place at the side of its counterpart; neither does it interact in the way the Naught of the Unconscious entered consciousness. There is no simple way to describe the union of the passing consciousness with the World, with Existence in its unchangeable presence. No "relation" can elucidate this union, as two totally other realms can not be related to each other, not even in exclusion. One can describe dimly what happens in saying that in the passing away and darkening of the subjective sphere objective Existence discloses its power and becomes illuminated. But it may be more adequate to speak in terms of action and to say: in its surrender and devotion, in the experience of sacrifice, life gets aware of Existence. It does not, however, get aware of it as an effect of its doing. For "causality" has to be discarded as an abstract device: Neither is the sphere of appearance a cause of existence, nor is existence a cause of the realm of appearances, as if it were a "thing in itself" hidden behind them. What we experience is, that our life runs its course in the presence of an Existence which gives it confidence and support; but which, on the other hand, denies itself to our fleeting experiences, as a future which never becomes a past, reminding us to give a meaning to our futility. In this way Existence shows two faces, and this has made it a mystery throughout the ages: We are apt to believe that Existence belongs to us, to all the appearances of our life, and so we call things "existent"; but on the other hand, we know that none of these things really exist, but that they reveal only in their passing away an existence which uses these things as occasions for its own disclosure. The things or essences are therefore not explained by existence, as if it were their predicate; nor are the essences in their turn predications of existence so that they would open existence to our understanding. The ambiguous nature of this mysterious existence is seen in the fact that appearances lose their self-sufficient character in the presence of existence, but that they win a new status as if "created" by existence, created out of their state of nothingness, "creatio ex nihilo." These things are however to be regarded as created merely in so far as they disclose existence, not in their essential and symbolic abstract nature. It would therefore be misleading to regard them as symbolizing existence: they are with regard to existence less and more than symbols: less, because they do not anticipate and fulfill existence; more, because instead of merely intending, they disclose existence in their passing away. The Middle Ages spoke here of "contingency," whereby however the thing was not contingent "as existing," as if existence as such were a contingency, but "as disclosing existence." [16] Our fleeting life in its probable course is contingent, when seen under the fateful power of an unchanging future, which, denying itself to the passing experiences, makes them slide backwards into the past and lose themselves in its darkness. We may call this unchanging future "Eternity," not as a timeless medium of Platonic ideas, but as an Eternity which as the ground and meaning of temporal events accompanies them and stretches beyond.

Time, however, is not "in Eternity," just as man is not "in the World." These spatial terms of accidental location are misleading. Life, consciousness, events and things unfold toward the World, supported by it and dependent upon it, shaken by fear and hope, contingent with regard to its existential necessity. But, indeed, in using the term "necessity" we fall back upon the sphere of abstraction, where necessity is relative to its possibilities, while existence is absolute and in no relation. Did we grant here too little to existence, we may have granted too much, when we spoke of it as "creating." We will have to consider the problem of creation later. It suffices here to mention, that a creative power lives in its creatures, while existence remains aloof, as much as we may experience its response to our aspirations. Religion has taken hold of the mystery of existence and has deified its power. But existence in its darkness may be the night in which the Divine spark is kindled, as the Mystics say, but it is not itself divine.

The ambiguous character of man in the face of a fateful existence, its hiddenness on the one hand and its disclosure on the other hand, all the paradoxes connected with this contradictory atmosphere of knowing and not-knowing, have given birth to a highly imaginative but playful structure: "Mythology." Mythology is an intermediate between the unbalancedness of life as appearance and a life which has conquered reality on the height of religion, ethics and art. In Mythology all findings are ambivalent, they give security, but they destroy it at the same time; they would shake man in exaltation and despair, if in the face of fate these contradicting moods were not balanced by resignation, by a surrender to "Fate." It is fate as a mythical necessity which rules over man's accidental life, and the accidents "disclose" the necessity not as instances disclose a law, but as signs, as vestiges of an overpowering existence. Every thing, every event is such a vestige, an "expression" of fate. "Expression" has here taken the place of symbol and image. Things and events are in themselves nothing, they have meaning only in disclosing fate, in "expressing" fate, that is: they are not possibles over against a necessity, they do not intend or anticipate anything, they simply express with immediacy fate in its concreteness. But, on the other hand, they do not exhaustively disclose existence ever, they only somehow hit upon it and somehow miss it; the expression does not ever equal the "expressed," it remains a—more or less—deficient, playful and accidental disclosure which not only asks for various interpretations, as Myths are indeed in need of interpretation, but which makes the expressions turn into each other, slip into ever other forms and show their highly ambivalent character. Fate is revealed as well as hidden in its expressions, discloses itself in them and denies itself to them, and so these expressions fulfill and fail, give security and threaten. Man may go to rest in either of those concrete forms, but he may just as well flee from them. Time and space are, wherever grasped, in every moment and in every place, holy as well as unholy. Thus man may resign in an impotent contemplation, in order to reach through the changing expressions into the ground and go to rest in Nirvana; he may, like a Buddhist, look at the vestiges as a mere illusion, rather hiding than revealing the ground. But if he is an active and scheming creature, he will, instead of resigning, try to build a structure of defense against threat and fear, he will separate, through an imposed pattern, what was ambivalent, separate the holy from the unholy, the white from the black, stabilize his environment and thus master it, providing security for himself and his neighbors. In this way the fleeting realm of Mythology is transformed into a rigid pattern of routine, into a reliable system of "Ritual," and it is done by a device which we may call "Magic."

But Magic and Ritual do not provide truth; they sacrifice truth for the sake of an easy security, they destroy whatever truth the Myth may have presented and expressed. They simply subject fate to an artificial device, make it harmless and, closing their eyes in the face of its unbearable power, believe to have found a remedy against its dangers. Thus Magic and Ritual blind man instead of making him see. Man has to reach beyond Mythology; but this is not done by closing the Myth into a rigid armour of ritual and by feigning magical knowledge. The playful relief which Myth provides, besides threatening, is not an adequate coping with reality, but neither is the artificial security of a magical pattern. Existence, when truly faced is dynamic and reaches into man's life as his "destiny." Man has to receive it with an open mind. Existence is "given" to consciousness of man, but it is not given as a content, not as something to be mastered and possessed, not even in the way in which "expression" possesses: It is independent, absolute and remains even when given in an infinite distance. Man is indeed here faced by reality which is given to him as a knower, but it is given only in order to make the knower realize his inability to understand, to really know and really possess in his knowledge. It is given to him as unknowable, as a mystery, and so the shadow of a tragic limitation falls upon the knower who can neither conquer reality nor reject it. In this situation the knower is shaken by a desire which drives him beyond his half-answers and keeps him on the never-ending road of his search. In vain he may try to find peace in finite answers, his infinite desire will drive him forever on. It is not to be wondered that rationalism escaped this tragedy by changing the infinite desire for the Unknowable into a finite desire for "the totality of the Known."

This metaphysical desire for existence, reaching out into infinity, will throw man into a state more forceful, but also more tragic, than the ups and downs of his mood had prepared him for. He will try to force the closed door open, he will knock impatiently against the wall which hides the Unknowable from his sight and he will not easily resign himself to the fact that the Unknowable is "given" to his knowledge only in order to make him aware of his impotence. That the Unknowable is "given" to knowledge may seem a paradox, but no more so than that the Unconscious should become an element in and for consciousness. In both cases we are at the mercy of a mysterious power: knowledge as well as consciousness at the mercy of either the Unknown or the Unconscious, possessed by this power instead of possessing; and it is here, in Desire, that we can speak of "passion." For passion is the subjection, the surrender and suffering with regard to a power which overwhelms and exposes us to the threat of insecurity and loss. Passion is the violent whipping up of our emotion under the threat of an irretrievable loss. When this overwhelming experience was expressed in religious terms, man spoke of the Divine power not as known, but as "knowing us," not as possessed, but as possessing us and as "revealing itself as hidden."

Desire is driven toward an objective which it does not possess but which possesses it and which provides it in spite of its ignorance with a firm direction. In our daily life and its small desires we seem to enjoy full knowledge of our objective and we seem to conquer it. But the fact that none of these conquests satisfies, but sends us again on our way, shows that we have fooled ourselves and that behind all these seeming conquests is an unconquered objective which keeps our desire alive and passionately devoted in spite of the pseudofulfillments at the wayside. No achievement and no answer which we possess allows us to come to rest; we are driven by question and doubt, and it is our desire for the ultimate which although hidden keeps us on the road. That desire never fully possesses and knows, was an insight which Plato already had, and he was right in stating that desire ends when we fully know and in knowing possess; but he was wrong in identifying this vanishing desire with love. Also this infinite desire will vanish as a passion, when its objective is reached—reached, however, not by means of abstraction, but "known" in a very specific way, and it will be this kind of knowledge on a higher level, which we will call "love," not transient, not vanishing in its fulfillment, but preserved in it forever. We will have to return to this problem, when we have reached the level where it presents itself.

The small fulfillments at the wayside leave us disappointed and make us continue our way, for they have only feigned to present us, in motive and purpose, the ultimate end we were seeking. Motives and purposes are only deficient interpretations and thus always to be corrected during the course of our life. The more narrow and the more superficial these motives and purposes are, the more easily do they lend themselves to understanding and fulfillment. The infinite desire which reaches beyond all of these and remains unfulfilled, cannot be closed in any motive or purpose; its objective surpasses all rational fixations. We may call this infinite desire our "Will," as it realizes but rejects the small achievements on its way. Thus the will may use the works done, the decisions made, it will use them but will not get stuck in them. It will feel its freedom in rising over these petty things, possessions, achievements; but it will be passionately devoted to and dependent on an objective which it cannot know and which holds the will in doubt and hesitation, in anxiety and hope. There is a certainty of direction which gives to the will courage and the dream of an absolute freedom. But this absolute freedom is an illusion on this level of a groping life, involved in its merely potential phases and never really rising above. Only when consciousness finds its union with the reality it is seeking, and is close to its World, will freedom too become a reality.

The insecurity, caused by the Unknowable, is responsible for "error." Error belongs essentially to the potential sphere. In the realm of abstraction errors may happen, but they have no root in abstraction itself, are foreign to a structure which firmly stands in its necessity. Error in the realm of abstraction is an accident, nothing more; it will be regarded as a merely psychological confusion, a slip of the mind, a lack of attention. But when the process of consciousness has detached itself from the embedding structure, has lost the protection which the abstract structure provided and has become exposed to existence, passionately devoted to and possessed by a desire for the unknown and unknowable, error becomes essential and even unavoidable. Descartes' infinite will, at odds with the finite intellect, and more even, Kant's tragic involvement of reason in a drive for infinity were insights into the fundamental nature of error. In his endeavor to know the Unknowable man will substitute his finite and deficient answers for the ultimate and unreachable truth and he will come to rest in these answers. But doubt may protect him and may reject with a stern "No" the erroneous answers, in order to keep the search open. Doubt serves a positive truth and is based on a belief in such a truth. The negation which it uses will equally be a means to protect the positive truth it serves. And here it may be permitted to say a word about negation as such. Negation is not "a speculative principle" as Hegel thought and not really creative. It keeps the road open for the positive and creative process of thought. Already the first negation we met, in the realm of Logic, was only a preparation for a positive statement: it was the relation of exclusion which led to inclusion and gave rise to the relation of identity. The negative proposition is similarly only a preparation for a positive proposition and protects against an impending danger of error. That in the sphere of the potential process error becomes a more immediate danger, is true, and so the negative proposition will in judgments of experience serve a more important role. Even here, however, it will be only a protection and prepare a positive insight. Also here the actual slip which leads to error will be conditioned by psychological causes, by a lack of concentration and attention. Nevertheless, the fact that in this realm insecurity rules, will make error more than a merely psychological accident; it is the dualism of levels which will make the negative proposition imperative and a necessary device of our reasoning in this field.

Thus it is not only the restlessness of emotion, but also the danger of error which made rationalists take refuge in symbolic structures and substitute them for the sinister existence. Since Parmenides and Plato essentialism has fought a successful battle against World and existence and has replaced both by a structure of abstraction. The drive for the infinite and unknowable reality was, however, not dismissed without a heavy price. For man, fenced into the prison of his finite purposes and forced into a routine of always-repeated devices, felt that life had lost its meaning and had become a curse. The myths of Sisyphus and of the Danaides are witness thereof.

Man cannot make his symbols into idols without facing a severe punishment. An idol is an abstract fixation, posing for reality and worshipped as such. Life becomes petrified in its idols, which are rendered into objects of obsession and infatuation. Passion and emotion are thus not really eliminated, but perverted and suppressed into the "unconscious," where they play havoc with life. A mild form of this perversion is found in the "hybris" of the Stoic Sage who identified himself with the idol of a total and perfect system of abstraction, deified and worshipped. Primitive religions have found simpler idolizations. Any object could serve as an idol and could turn the life of the tribe into a fixed ritual, arresting this life in mechanism and repetition. For here, as often, the sickness itself is called in as a physician and prescribes a medicine which instead of healing increases the sickness. The ritual in its repetitive pattern hardens instead of enlivening, and so the action which should free rivets on the fetters and intensifies the obsession.

This is not unlike the dreamlife, where the Unconscious as a motherly ground embeds the consciousness in its darkness, absorbs the will and arrests the process in content, which will assume a fixed and abstract structure. Freud has detected several abstract devices of the dream-structure, and has called them "condensation," "identification," "symbolization." The paradox of the dream, however, is that its play of abstraction does not provide the haven of security it was supposed to provide and which the monistic absorption of the process in its content would make us expect. The dream only feigns a fulfillment and results in frustration instead. We speak of "wish-dreams," but the wish appears only as a means to bring frustration into play.

In times of transition and insecurity man suffers most intensively from existence and its problems. Doubt and self-accusation darken life; the flight into sickness, into neurosis, becomes a necessity. Abnormal psychology will set the pace of our knowledge of man in such troubled times. The "idee fixe," compulsion and obsession will leave their mark on life, and man, fenced in by his dream-world, will lose contact with his fellowmen. There is much truth in the deeply depressing analyses of Sartre; but it would be wrong to regard them as the last word, elucidating human nature. What is described here is a pathological state of mind, as much as this may be a typical pathological state in certain periods of development.

The dualism which is difficult to bear and to overcome in times of weakness and which in such times results in pathological perversions, is an inevitable phase in the ascent to reality and by no means merely destructive. It can be creative too, when the desire for the Unknown leads over trial and error upward to an ever-increasing understanding. Desire is as such no knowledge, but a passionate urge for knowledge, for that ultimate knowledge, which is instinctively intended in all acts of learning, in all those acts, unsatisfactory in themselves, through and beyond which we strive for the Unknowable. Scholasticism knew that the Unknowable is not an object of the intellect, but that it is, sought for in God, an object of the will, of emotion. The attitude of the knower to the known would lack depth, if the desire for the Unknowable would not carry it forward, and would protect against our getting lost in immature and premature answers. The genius of the Scholar is marked by tragedy, by the tragic, never-resting desire for the unfulfillable. Escape from this tragedy is possible and will land man in the secure haven of a closed system. But, when the urge for ultimate truth is thus destroyed, man will become a skeptic and pessimist. He will know that he broke down on the road, and in his despair and defeat he might turn against his better self, he might accuse his will of being nothing but a freedom to err and to fail, and he might gladly renounce this freedom as a highly questionable gift of God.

VI. DESTINY AND FREEDOM

The problem of freedom presented itself at the end of the preceding chapter. It rose out of man's bitter awareness that he is left to himself in the face of Existence and that he is, in his independence, doomed to fail. Freedom appears here rather as an impotence than as a power, nearer to accident than to a firm directedness. The "negative freedom" to fail is indeed only a breach in the rule of necessity, law and abstraction, and thus an accident. And like all exceptions from the rule it confirms the rule from which it deviates. Negative freedom presupposes necessity and is finally a return to the necessity from which it broke away.

So the freedom to err is not much more than the dark side of rationalism, the symptom of a chaotic disorder beyond the fences of an idolized system, and thus it was indeed regarded by the Stoic sage. His freedom to err and to be entangled in emotions was a mere disorder, an accident, avoidable by total surrender to the system. But freedom as a breach of order can be much more than an accidental falling away from necessity. It can be an active aspiration to reach beyond the structure of necessity into a higher reality. As such it will start as a rebellion against abstraction. Rebellions, however, blinded by emotion, overreach themselves, and are apt to fail. Such a rebellion will underrate the power of its adversary; it may at best succeed by protecting man from a surrender to routine. But as negative freedom has no positive ideal and is concerned with nothing but the breaking of fetters, it will not know what to do with its freedom and will ultimately perish, leaving the victory to the very necessity it fought.

It is not a matter of chance that Greek civilization provides the most brilliant examples of a rebellious freedom. For it was in Greece that necessity as the goddess of "Dike" ruled, a mythical fate, rationalized by abstraction into law and order, but never totally domesticated. Fate as a divine power weighed heavily on the Greek mind, as much as it tried to lift the weight by an attempt of rationalization.

The Greek rebellion occurred in two forms: Its milder form was directed against the rationalized fate of law and assumed the character of Skepticism as a philosophy of withdrawal and suspense. The other, more powerful rebellion, was directly concerned with the mythical subjection of man to fate, and it found its immortal representation in Greek tragedy, where man struggled to preserve his freedom against a relentless power of law and necessity, mythically hypostatized as Fate.

These rebellions were certainly no mere escape. On the contrary, they faced their adversary courageously and tried to break his fetters. It was thus a straightforward and clean attitude. But it ended with defeat and confirmed the power which it had fought in vain. This is undeniable with regard to the rebellion of tragedy. It is an essential feature of tragedy that man is crushed by the power of fate which in its absoluteness and mysterious grandeur assumes the sublime character of a Divine order. Fate rules and destroys man and renders his freedom to Naught. Fate in tragedy is a power beyond life and consciousness, hostile to them; but this very fate is also linked to life, giving it its ultimate meaning, and as such life's "destiny." Destiny is fate, understood as concrete and individual in spite of its universal and dominant nature, reaching into the life of the hero, if only to destroy it. His destiny, however, belongs to the hero, he may even be proud of it, and although it lastly triumphs over his life and crushes it, he will say "yes" to his own destruction and by yielding to it he will confirm its power. Even when the rebel seems to break his fetters and to free himself from his prison, the broken fetters will still remain with him, and all his life will be a flight from the prison he left, directed and ruled by the very power he broke. Negative freedom is no freedom, but a detour to necessity and law, strengthened by a defeated rebellion.

The freedom of the skeptic, the freedom of suspense, is also in the end defeated, seeking security in convention. Various forms of this attempted freedom have kept thinkers in a troubled state. The so-called "freedom of indifference" is one of these modes of negative freedom. Man cannot, however, remain for long in this indifference; the suspense is meaningless and felt rather as an unfreedom than as a freedom. Sooner or later the indifference has to yield to some kind of a position; every position will be hailed as a liberation from the suspense; every "fait accompli" will be welcome, and it may be a totally accidental fact which in this way relieves the strain of indifference. The freedom of indifference has its most famous application as the "freedom to choose." This mode of a negative freedom badly hides the fact that it is no freedom at all. It is here quite obvious that this so-called freedom is only a transitional state, that it has to end in something which contradicts it: the freedom to choose is already, while it lasts, overshadowed by the "necessity to choose." The chooser cannot possibly remain in his freedom to choose; he is forced to end this freedom by a decision. And while he is in the state of choosing, he feels the necessity to end it by a decision, as if a doom were hanging over him. He may even regard himself as unfree because his empty negative freedom makes it impossible for him to come to a decision. Buridan's ass starved in this situation and not merely because he was an ass. The empty fredom to choose is indeed a doom, and it was this doom of emptiness which entered modern theories of freedom as expounded by Sartre, the freedom of nothingness as a curse.

Resignation was therefore the result of the breaking down of a negative freedom, whether of a freedom of rebellion or of indifference. This resignation to a fate which rules our lives entered the Christian era and was understood as surrender and devotion to the Divine will: predestination is the Augustinian answer and the ultimate end of human freedom; man can only say "freely" yes to the power which rules, condemns and crushes his life. This predestination was rationalized further by Calvinism and was interpreted as a Divine judgment for which reasons had to be found in the facts of human life, so that the fateful necessity became somehow bearable for man who wanted to know why he was condemned. But resignation remained the last residue of a freedom which was reduced to the ability of man to understand his doom.

It is this resignation, made bearable by human consent, which is also at the bottom of Heidegger's surrender to fate. Here fate is illustrated by the unconquerable power of death, the only "unsurpassable" possibility of life, as Heidegger calls it. Death is a necessity which condemns and crushes life, the most terrifying fate, because it renders life meaningless. But just because of that we have "freely" to give meaning to death, we have, like the tragic hero, to say "yes" to our own destruction and to make it the crowning fact of our existence. We have, if our life is to be "authentic," to live toward death intentionally, as if death were our free decision. But since death is a necessity beyond our control, such a "free" decision is rather a fiction of freedom, a surrender to fate under the disguise of freedom.

True freedom, if there is such a thing, will have to rise above death as above all mere facts or possibilities in our life. Death is indeed a fact in life, and life has to rise above this as above all the facts contained in its course. Death may be found in every station on our way: every time we stop and come to rest we take leave and acknowledge that an end has been reached. But although this is so, it is essential for life that none of these ends is "the" end, that life rises out of every end, that death has its resurrection, as the old gave birth to the new in the infinite course of imagination.[1] Maybe, that the imaginative veiling of death, its dimming down in the unconscious, is what Heidegger objects against in the life of every-day imagination, and that he asks for a conscious and intentional confrontation with death. But such a confrontation rendering death to a content of consciousness would result only in resignation, as in Greek tragedy, in Calvinistic predestination, and so here in the conscious stagnation and arrest in the fate of death. As a mere resignation the arrest in an inescapable fate is no solution of freedom, but rather a restoration and return to the world of Myth, where man—under the impact of fate—is entangled in the ambivalence of events, holy and unholy, salvation and condemnation, life and death, all irretrievably intermingled and leaving man utterly confused.

Negative freedom is only a transition, belonging to the transitional realm of appearance and imagination. It is—at best—a storm-signal, announcing the advent of a better truth. As all negations it is a preparation only and relative to something else which it discloses as resisting to it. Science has, indeed, to work with such relative entities, with energies, growing according to the resistance they meet, to the mass which corresponds to their merely relative power. A truly free power would have to create its own resistance, as the Leibnizian monad, the Fichtian Ego and the God of Genesis.

Absolute freedom, if there is anything of this kind at all, is not a negative freedom, a "freedom from." But it can neither be a "freedom for," a freedom to achieve something and to realize a fixed purpose. A purpose is again only an abstract structure of necessity and would assume the character of fate, ruling over a life, devoted to its realization. Who gives himself to a "cause"—even to a "great cause"—makes this cause to the law which dominates him and deprives him of freedom. Besides: No cause is the ultimate cause, but merely a station on the road. Even the realm of abstraction could not culminate in "the end," the "purpose" as its peak of achievement, but had to launch into the mystery of "force," closed to abstraction.[2]

Neither "freedom from" nor "freedom for" is true freedom. In his despair man may take refuge to a "tour de force," to a tautology: He may believe to be free for—not any specific purpose, but—for freedom itself, free for the sake of freedom. But such a circle of identity is nothing but an escape into a jumble of words. Even when expressed in a more respectable form as the freedom of "selfrealization," it is still empty of meaning, unless selfrealization points to the perpetuation of life's infinite possibilites on the level of appearance and imagination. But this level should have been left behind and transcended, when faced by "existence" and the necessity of selfsurrender. Selfsurrender is a higher truth than selfrealization, but it is still only a preparation and transition, disclosing the fleeting character of life's ever new possibilities which remain possibilities, even when realized and lost in the past. Possibles of the future are still only possibles when changed to hard facts of the past, necessary when reflected upon, but in their seeming necessity still affected by accidentality, as the medium of appearance, and man, wavering between the possibles of future and past, will at the end resign, tired out by the impossibility of realizing the dream of free creativity.

History, the history of the individual as well as that of the race, has been darkened by the accidental character of its events and has led to Skepticism and Cynicism. It seemed a hopeless hunt after possibilities which when realized turned out to be nothing but illusions, insignificant when reflected upon as hardened facts of the past, meaningless in their accidental sequence. Historicism has often been blamed for the disillusionment and discouragement which follows in its wake.

But when History is interpreted in this way, abstraction has crept in with its modalities of "possibility" and "necessity," none of which has a real place in living history. What is omitted here is the true essential of history, not found in the "freedom for," introducing a final cause as a necesssity for possible realization, and neither found in the "freedom from," where again a necessity is raised, a fetter, which freedom in vain tries to break, as a prison, which continues to determine man even after he escaped: for the past is and remains here a necessity, from which man never really escapes into freedom.

When we consider history concretely and not in abstraction, neither possible nor necessary facts are the constituent elements. A new category has here to be discovered which expresses the direction of life as an unfolding of a meaning not detached from the process of activity, not placed as purpose in the way of this activity, entering from outside and limiting its scope, but present as attitude in the awareness of those who carry the process of history, an attitude which is its own fulfillment. It is this attitude which is the reality in history, the ground and the achievement, not any sequence of facts which will only inadequately manifest the attitude of historical men. There will of course be also abstract causes, purposes, thrown ahead, anticipated and carried out in the service of that concrete inner attitude which determines history. But these abstract and fixed goals are only tentative interpretations, approximations never fully doing justice to the truth which lives in the people; and therefore these goals, these fixed and abstract patterns have to be perpetually corrected and taken back into the living course. We may speak vaguely of a certain "tact" which inspires historical man and gives him the direction to be followed, an inspiration which cannot be put into any repeatable pattern of law. Therefore the meaning of history has, as a unique meaning, to be dug out of the very facts, and it is the genius of the historian to detect it, to select and emphasize those facts which are most representative for this meaning. In Science facts provide us with information relating to unchanging and timeless laws; in history facts are the manifestation of unrepeatable, unique developments, and the interest in these developments is not the general validity of a pattern, but the validity of a unique meaningful unfolding of a devotion which we share and which intensifies the direction of our own lives.

The truth which lives in historical people is, of course, no mere dream. It drives people into action, and it is this action, imbued with a lived truth, which is "historical action." Only facts which are shaped by such a truth are historical facts. We may call the unfolding of the truth in facts shaped by it, and meaningful as an unfolding, the "progress in history." Men have ridiculed the idea of progress because they took progress for a scientific assumption, inferred from the facts as instances of a law. There is no "law of progress," however, for the progress has its reality in the attitude of the people, and its truth-value is not affected by success or failure in carrying it out. Historical man is convinced of his truth, which lives in him and for which he is ready to die, whether the facts confirm it or not. The truth of this progress is twofold: it is an objective truth, not an arbitrarily and subjectively adopted truth, discovered by the devotee as an inner necessity; and it is besides a responsibility to make it "come true" in historical facts. The prophets of history, the religious as well as the profane, have therefore pronounced their truth of progress as a revelation of reality, but at the same time they have instigated men to become bearers of this progress. Their truth was revealed as unquestionable and objective, but this revealed objective truth had to become the responsibility of those who were devoted to it in order that it might "come true." This seemed a paradox and a ridiculous contradiction to unbelievers. But it is, in fact, the way in which progress as an objective direction must at the same time be a subjective doing of responsible men. Responsibility rises out of history as a making and a revelation at once. It is a mysterious problem, to be discussed later.

The unbelievers have ridiculed the idea of progress because they did not know that in this sphere truth is an objective reality of "Faith." We use here the word Faith rather than belief, for faith emphasizes the absolute reality and objectivity of its truth. One does not "have" this faith, however, as one "has" a possession, not even in the way in which knowledge of facts or laws is "had." There is no faith in facts or laws, they are simply known. Faith is an attitude with regard to something not known, not possessed, not even as a purpose or a desire. Faith points to a future, as desire does, and as purpose does in its anticipation; but faith as an attitude is a present which governs the future, not merely anticipates or longs for it. It is the reality of a future which merely brings into the open what has been concretely realized already in the attitude of faithful man. Faith, although not possessing its object in the way which knowledge does, and not possessed by its object as desire is, is closer and more intensely united with it than knowledge or desire, which at any time may drop or lose their objects. The object of faith cannot be dropped or lost, it is alive in the faithful, it is his own reality and Being, and his responsible action follows from this faith as a mere manifestation. To put it into one single word: Faith is a "Force," and as the presence of force it includes, as a present, its future, manifesting itself in this future as an unfolding progress, objective in this future because of the perpetual presence of the force, in spite of the subjective working of willing, thinking and reflecting men which carry the faith into responsible action.

We have met the idea of "Force" in the abstract realm and even in Science, but as a foreign element, scorned by purists of abstraction. Science wants to observe and infer. But force is neither observed as facts are, nor inferred as laws. The scientific idea of force was "suggested" merely as a "why," as an ideal of truth and meaning behind the laws in their hypothetical deficiency. In history Force is not merely suggested and not introduced as an ideal, it is experienced with immediacy and is concretely present in the faith which conveys its own reality to the facts, making them into "historical facts," meaningful beyond their merely causal sequence. The force which lives as faith in man gives universality to the facts, gathers them up in the meaning of a validity more absolute than any abstract law, because it is not merely deduced from the facts but instrumental and responsible for their being. That these facts can also be reflected upon scientifically and be brought under causal laws is true, but if we stop at this stage of reflection, then we merely gather material for timeless necessities and receive information with regard to "human nature" as such, or "political behavior" as such; but we miss the unique meaning which makes history a field of its own, and distinguishes it from natural science. In history facts are real beyond their abstract necessity, revealing a Force which gave them existence and which rises above the facts and situations.

Life, as the potential process of imagination, builds on facts as history does, but it approaches its anticipated goals in probable steps, shaken by doubt and hesitation. In history goals may also be thrown ahead, tentatively adopted, but these goals and their factual realization are not the reality in history. The reality is the faith, as a force, not probable, but an objective, infallible and unwavering attitude. That the facts, as they follow in causal sequence or as the realization of final causes, may fail to fulfill the reality of faith, is true but does not affect the faith itself which is not dependent on the happenings, accidental in the light of the faith itself. These happenings may, in spite of their causal necessity, be called "possible" with regard to the meaning of a living faith, and this faith in its turn may be called "necessary." But if we use these terms, we must be aware that this use is really inadequate outside the abstract sphere. Possibility and necessity are modalities which belong to the same level and are related to each other mutually. But faith as a force is not on the same level with its manifestation in facts. We have therefore to use another term in order to characterize the force of faith, as beyond a mere necessity of its facts, and it is here that the term "Freedom" finds its place. The faith which lives in man is a "free force," real in its independent present and manifesting this presence in future facts which receive their meaning from the free force and its all-encompassing presence. Thus the force of faith is indeed "free for" but not for any fixed goal which subjects it, but free for the realization of facts which manifest its "power."

The term "Power" lends itself easily to our use, when we characterize the force as the dominating source of its factual manifestations. For "power" is a word which preserves the familiar terms possibility and necessity, and compromises with them as they have been sanctified by abstraction. "Power" expresses a necessity which carries its own possibilities as its manifestations. Power is free, for none of its dependent and—when seen in the light of its forceful necessity—accidental manifestations can determine or alter the free power itself. Power should not be confounded with the "probable necessity" of life and its doubtful unfolding, dependent on an existence as a fate hovering over it. Vitalism has at times, posing as a philosophy of life, usurped the idea of "power," as Nietzsche did. Power in its true meaning, however, was discovered, if only dimly, in the energy and entelechy of Aristotle and in the "One" of Plotinus, and it found its full recognition in the Will of St. Augustine, for whom "omnis est voluntas."

The free living power of faith is beyond the abstract structure of law which, as hypothetical, receives absoluteness and justification in its service to an unfolding and progressing force. It becomes a "disposition" for this free unfolding; it is not destroyed, but confirmed by the free force and its working. Thus freedom takes the order of abstraction under its wing, for there is no competition between the two realms, no hostility as a misguided rebellion assumed. The structure of abstraction becomes the scaffold, indispensable for the carrying out of the free force throughout its manifestation.

Only those who are arrested in the idolization of the abstract sphere may regard the serving role of abstraction as an unbearable dethronement, and may violently resist this subjection. From their point of view the world of necessity and laws is, indeed, in opposition and has to resist the free power which appears as a usurper. The theory which regards the free force as a breaker of resistance has to be rejected and is due to abstraction itself and its method of explaining by negation and exclusion; just as the Given of space-time was regarded by abstraction as negating the things and happenings in its orbit, and just as Existence seemed to a life, structured in phases of abstract appearance, to be a threat of destruction. There will always be an estrangement where abstraction builds on exclusion and negation, and this estrangement will not be healed even if the excluded elements are assimilated to each other in order to be related in exclusion.[3] For the sake of exclusion the structure of abstraction may assume here the character of a force too, a resisting force, and it will now be this pseudo-force of the abstract structure which as the "force of the intellect" seems to compete with the "force of the will." But if this is done, the force of Will, as a breaker of resistance, is made dependent on its adversary, loses its freedom and becomes highly problematic. The greatest thinkers have tried to reconcile law and freedom, intellect and will. Aristotle imbued his energy with a lawful "telos" and called it "Entelechy," understanding profoundly the integration of necessity and freedom; but his unity was often misinterpreted as a onesided emphasis on the telos to which the process of activity seemed subjected. Even more misleading was Kant's attempt to compromise between law and will in his ethics, where the free will seemed to be subjected to the "moral law" and could be saved only by the acknowledgement that the dominating law was not really a law but only its form.

The necessary law structure and the free will are not in any competition, because they belong to different levels. The "intellect" may present a relational manifold of alternatives to the will: but these alternatives are neither an obstacle for freedom, nor do they constitute it. That freedom is not constituted by an alternative of choice, was stated above.[4] But it would be equally wrong to regard the structure of alternatives, presented in the necessary balance of its possibilities, as an obstacle which freedom has to overcome. The free will uses this intellectually patterned structure, the "situation," as its disposition which receives meaning through the will and its direction, and serves as a scaffold for the free decision. Only weak men get stuck in the alternatives, hesitate, waver to and fro, and finally are lost. But the strong person knows that the situation is merely a disposition of the will, a situation which the will has to shape by giving it a new meaning. The "decision" is the realization of this new meaning and therefore entirely dependent on the will itself which had shaped the situation. It is erroneous to think that by a decision any one of the alternatives is chosen at the expense of the others, picked out of an assortment offered to the will. The alternatives which the intellect offered in a relational manifold are welded by the will into a unity which is neither identical with any one of the alternatives nor with the sum total of them, as they were presented in abstraction. What the decision takes hold of and brings to its realization is a new entity, created by the will, perhaps using hereby these alternatives, perhaps drawn by them into a totally different direction, but always free in its shaping. Therefore not only "choice" is absent, but also hesitation and doubt. Alternatives, motives as f.i. needs or wants may enter the decision of the will, but only after they have undergone the transformation into dependent elements of the situation which is the will's situation, as a material only and in the role which the will allows them to play. Needs are independent necessities in the field of biology, but not here where they have become indistinguishable factors in the situation. And this situation does not "cause" the decision: causality rules among the elements of the situation, not between situation and will. Thus the situation is not a mere material, given externally to the will: it is the will's situation, belonging to the will and responding to it, rising at times even to an inspirational factor of the will which is acting. We shall return to this significant nature of the "material," when coping with the phenomenon of Art. Here we may be content to mention that causality of need or any such motivation has its place neither in art nor in ethics nor in religion. Surely, the believer feels a "need" for God, the lover a longing for the beloved, the reader or spectator a craving for something which may rid him of emptiness. But these needs are not constitutive for religion, ethics or art. If these realms depended on the fulfillment of needs, they would end in this fulfillment, as sexual love does, as superstitious religion ends in mere comfort, and as play, not art, ends in "entertainment" as the elimination of boredom. Plato indeed thought that love was transitional and ended in the fulfillment of a need. But we know better. Needs determine biology, resistance physics—but neither of them determines religion, ethics and art.

The absence of motive and purpose, of any kind of causation in the working of a free power has been widely recognized. But the mystery which seemed to cloud such an uncaused power was unbearable to those who were arrested in abstract thought. So the attempt was made to substitute for the unbearable mystery an absurd and highly dangerous causation: the absence of purpose was now understood as a purpose itself, the absence of motive was made itself a motivation. Just as in rational theology the absence of cause with regard to God led to the absurd "causa sui," so the absence of purpose led to a "power for the purpose of power," or to a "power for power's sake." Behind these seemingly harmless identifications of reason loomed a dangerous and destructive activity. If power fulfilled its purpose by intensifying itself, then it had to suppress everything which might stand in the way of this power. Thus power was forced into a fanatic activity which it had to carry out: it had to destroy purposes and the people who were devoted to these purposes. For efficiently doing this, power had to organize its activity, and so institutions were set up with the purpose of intensifying their power by destroying whatever seemed an obstacle, because it had a purpose of its own. Power-organizations sprang into life, designed for the sole purpose of suppressing the life and activity of those who were their chief responsibility. Had the theory of God as "causa sui" been carried through consistently—which it never was—then such a God would have been at least indifferent to anything which was not himself. But when power became not only its cause but its own purpose, it turned violently against everything that could possibly limit it. So persecution and tyranny became the absurd results of this caricature of freedom. The "almighty" organization expanded its own emptiness into a destructive, aggressive, and ultimately self-defeating activity.

If we ask: why has history so often failed in spite of the sincere and honest yearning for progress, then the explanations usually given are not sufficient. The greed and lust for pleasure, the egoistic nature of man are not strong enough to account for the hardships, yes, the martyrdom which men took upon themselves for the sake of power. The person who lives and dies for nothing but power is a tragic person, infatuated by an idol which eats his substance away and makes him suffer, and at last perish in the service to this idol. It is a misplaced devotion, directed in sacrifice to an empty idol, which has been responsible for the terrible errors, bloody and murderous, in the course of history. That history appears as a "slaughter-bench," to use Hegel's term, is not an essential fact of human history but its perversion. Certainly this perversion had its reasons; it was grounded in an idea of freedom which, unable to transform the structure of necessity and imbue it with life, found its purpose in destroying it, destroying any purposive set-up which it regarded as an obstacle, absurdly using the technique provided by the very object it fought. Organizations were set up and expanded, possessions were amassed, wealth became an obsession; and man forgot to ask whether they served any purpose at all. How could such a question be asked in an atmosphere where purposes were their own means of destruction? History, in the moment when it had discovered its meaning as a progressive and creative power, in the Christian era, was poisoned by a madness which turned truth into a lie and resulted in a witches' sabbath worse than any that had ever before existed in more ignorant times. Imperialism, which had been naive in former periods, became a devilish drive for unlimited power, for a "progress" which ate away the faith by which it had been nourished.

If in such a tribulation mankind did preserve a last spark of faith, this was due to a phenomenon, which may throw new light on our problem. Abstract power may have ruled over the course of history, but in the heart of the people the guide was a faith, directed toward a concrete person which embodied the ideal of progress in its purity better than any abstract purpose could have done, and which protected against the madness of an empty idol of power. Man enshrined their ideal in a person they loved, adored and adopted as a guide on their way to progress. Such a person may have been a hero grown to legendary stature, it may have been a saint, or even God Himself. The great history narrated in the Bible is the history of a people who embodied their faith in progress in the love and service of their God. This service was not always carried out, there were deviations, for example the adoration of the golden calf and other idols. But even these deviations became historical facts by being subjected to the one and only standard of this history: faith and service to the abundant life of God. We may therefore conclude that what restored faith and kept mankind on the road to progress in spite of innumerable disasters and treacheries, was the embodiment of progress in a personality. Only when persons realize their future in the possibilities which another, greater life opens to them can freedom, as a positive and creative power, be preserved.[5]

In the communion of life with life our will is directed, not to an object which in its fixation encroaches upon those who are confronted by it, but toward a life which responds. Wherever the possibility in us meets a necessity, fixed and objectified in this fixation, our freedom is endangered by the object which, as a purpose, determines the course of our life. But when our free activity is drawn to a life, this life, itself a free possibility, will not determine, not necessitate, but will "respond." We were faced with a dim response in the realm of appearance, where "Nature" responded to our emotions; but this response was a reflection of our emotional longing and was darkened by our questionable, apparent and imaginative status, separated by an abyss from the responding power which remained a fateful necessity held apart from man in awe and even anxiety. Existence broke into life from above and beyond as an unattainable object of desire, a never fulfillable future. Here, however, this very Existence reveals itself as a future united with him who desires, and meaningful through this communion. It is not anxiety which here separates life from a power, strange and violent. On the contrary, the future is here perpetually created by a faith in a life toward which this faith is directed and for which it feels itself responsible; and it is this other life which in its turn responds to our faith by providing it with ever new tasks, new possibilities, not limiting but widening our power abundantly and inexhaustibly. The other life becomes the everready incentive for the intensification of our life. So not only is the object of faith renewed in every moment but also the faithful subject himself. Here is, in fact, no subject confronted by an object which stands over against it and limits its action; here is rather a subject in communion of life with another subject, both enhancing mutually their freedom and transforming power. What seems a necessity in the other, his character, his "nature," turns out to be an opportunity for creation, realized in the communion and enriching the creator. In this way necessity is perpetually transformed into possibility; and both lives—in a unity which is neither identity nor difference, but a dynamic "sharing,"—are held together and held apart on a level of depth, intensity and fulfillment which we call "Love."

Only in this sharing of love is man truly "free for." To be "free for" does not mean here to be directed to a fixed object which in its necessity of structure becomes the determining goal, the "end" in which freedom indeed would come to an end. On the contrary, the free person is directed toward and is a possibility for a life which being free itself responds as a possible, intensifies the possibility of the other, and so grows together with this other life in abundance and resourcefulness. Each of these free forces rises out of a structure of necessity, a situation, but each transforms this necessity into a free possibility for the other.

This directedness of Will toward another will, this opening up in free communion and mutual response is what makes a "Personality." Any definition of Personality is unsatisfactory. All that can be done, and all that we should try to do, is to give a place to Personality in the course of our work and to elucidate its meaning by pointing to the way in which it is achieved. Personality is the only free force, essentially directed to and living in a communion and mutual response with another Personality. Personality is more than a conscious self. It does not have an environment of things over against it which, by questioning and doubting and by a subjective endeavor to know, it tries to master, itself unstable and in need of purpose and law. All this it uses in its own way; but it transforms this environment, makes it a mere opportunity, gives it meaning, and subjects it to its own reality which is the reality of communion and love. The realm of things becomes in this way more than a mere appearance and is justified as the starting-ground and disposition for the free working of Personalities.

The communion of life with life is not a "relational structure." A relation is a device of abstraction in which the terms are fixed and kept separate in this fixation in spite of their relatedness; and so are the "symbols" which stand for truth and are, by so much, related. Personality is not "relative;" it is absolute and it "symbolizes" no truth other than itself. It is its own truth, incomparable, a World in itself but not closed like a system. It is open to the life which it shares. We may speak of "sharing" in different ways. We share an object, a possession, and in such a sharing two people may be "related" in the full sense of the term, united through the object which they share in spite of their difference. But the sharing we are concerned with here is quite another thing. Here no object is present to provide unity; here lives as such in their infinite richness are shared, and no specific and limited interest could be pointed out in which and because of which they meet. There is no "reason" for their union, not even a specific quality in one of them which is instrumental for their mutual responses. It is the totality of the one Personality with all its tendencies and possibilities of the future which unites in a total communion with all the tendencies and resources of the other. Such a totality of infinite resources cannot be defined and conceptually differentiated, and consequently it cannot be fixed in a relation of difference from any other entity. But it would be equally impossible to regard both lives as identical, destroying by such an identity the creative communion of possibilities for each other. Inasmuch as Personality is grounded in a structure of necessity, in the situation of its body or, closer to the core of Personality, in its "character," these personality-structures can, as different, be reflected upon and related. But when these structures have been transformed and have as dispositions given rise to free possibilities of creation and response, no difference does justice to the person and the unity of its communion.

All this is obvious, if we keep in mind that the person with whom we are in communion is not a "content" of our consciousness and cannot, like a content, be judged and conceptually clarified. Personality is not consciousness of content and has not another personality over against it as its object, as a knower has his known. In the sharing of life with life no contingent content is detached from the process of life in its abundance. It is this abundance itself which is personality and structure at once, constituted in the free communion where no content, no purpose or motive necessitates.

It is here in the communion of person with person, therefore, that the problem of the conscious and the unconscious receives a new answer. On the level of appearance and imagination our consciousness was dimmed down and lost in the content which stood out as conscious before the darkened ground; and although we emphasized that consciousness rises out of its death again, living meant, as Heraclitus knew, a perpetual dying. Even when confronted with World, with Existence, consciousness was darkened by passion, blinded in the struggle, in fear and hope separated from and united with a distant reality, involved in things and their mastery. Only here in the communion of person with person the "consciousness of direction" beyond content, beyond things, as an unbroken consciousness, preserves itself and so the person is "conscious of himself" through and in interaction with the other. Self-consciousness is not a consciousness of self as an object and content, but of self as directed force, revealed in communion. Only in the communion of love is the "Γνῶθι Σεαυτον" of the Delphic god realized, but not under the guidance of this god, rather under the guidance of a God of love, through whose auspices self-consciousness is realized in the service to another life. Here every shadow of the unconscious is dispersed by the light of the communion. Man may fall back into darkness when he ignores the life of others and is walled up in his power and might, setting up organizations for destruction, spreading death around him and in himself and perishing in blind fury, ending in the night of the unconscious.[6] But when life has found its meaning in another life, not as content, possessing it, but as a direction and source of creativity, no unconscious urge darkens its course. The unconscious will still play its role in the content where appearance and imagination, the structure of motives and needs, become the material by which the will rises above its situation, and because of which passion and error will occur. There, in this situation, relational limitation and symbolic differentiation will lead to conceptual elucidation, and so the character will emerge as different, fenced in by its self-identity. The communion of personalities, however, will defy any relational differentiation or identification. It will build on a differentiation of character, but it will transcend it.

After having ruled out, however, all mere "relations" and with them all "abstract difference" among personalities, the problem of "personal incomparability" becomes the more vital. No doubt: the more incomparable a person is, the more he is open to the communion and the more intensely tied to other persons. The Individual, not the type, is the incentive for a loving understanding. We have to find, therefore, a specific term which expresses the incomparability, opening up to others in spite of its closedness. This specific term is the "Unique." Every person is "unique," and this uniqueness is, although absolute, unique "for another," in communion with another equally unique person, who experiences, shares and understands this uniqueness. Nobody is unique with regard to himself. And furthermore: "Unique" is an attribute of persons only, not of things, and the understanding of a person is the knowing of its uniqueness. While knowing of things consists in knowing their typical and lawful behavior, the "knowing of uniqueness" is not fixed and factual, but a "faith in" a life, experienced in a dynamic sharing, aspiration and response.

To "know" and to "have faith" are two different attitudes. We "know" in the proper sense the character as fixed and factual, stable in its systematic interrelation of qualities. But we "have faith" in the personality which perpetually develops and changes the character in spite of its fixedness. The character is finite, limited and its actions are "probable" and in so far predictable. But its fixation is perpetually pushed out of its fences, widened and corrected by the working of the personality and its communion of love and responsibility.

Here we may return for a moment to the problem of Consciousness versus "World," the subject versus "Existence," darkened by fear, and the shadow of the Unknowable.[7] In the communion of love it is the responding life which reveals a World and guarantees reality and existence; and our first and fundamental insight into reality is the awareness of life in which we share: It is so with the infant who grasps in the smile of its mother for the first time an existence, a reality, and from this moment on reality, world, existence will be grounded in the living communion of personalities. How could we ever know with certainty the reality of fellowmen, if this reality were not the foundation of our own life, the communion as an immediate, fundamental experience of Being. This is not a metaphor, but a metaphysical truth, elucidating the dim awareness of world and existence as they presented themselves in the sphere of a potential vitalism.

Who is closed against this reality in a solipsism of his character is therefore doomed to a perpetual irreality. Unable to transcend himself and the fixation of his character, he will be arrested as to direction and development and will be lost in the Unconscious, while the fixed content will prescribe and necessitate an unfree and limited field of action, repeated in a mechanical and ever more petrified routine. Cut off from devotion and communion as the constitutive ground of personality, such a man will be walled up in himself, in "self-love" and "self-realization," he will fructify his talents, his nature and will turn perpetually to this his own lawful and necessary possession, hardening in repetitive actions, arrested in the narrow fences of his disposition. In exploiting his own possibilites he will become barren, using himself as a thing, a possession, and thus misunderstanding and debasing his own nature, just as he will use and exploit and debase others. Estrangement will isolate him, isolation will change into suspicion and hostility, and so he will end up as an enemy not only to others but also to himself. In spite of its seeming necessity such a life will be ruled by accidents, for the "nature" of man, seen from the perspective of personality and its transforming power, is accidental, when estranged from the creativity of the communion. If the "nature," the biological and psychological endowment of man, were not accidental with regard to the person, man could not transform it and could not be regarded as responsible for his life. The "self-lover" indeed, is scarcely responsible; he is a pathological case, a routine-mechanism.

Whoever studies only the "nature of man," the character isolated as a factual system of law, will not do justice to personality. A psychology which limits its studies to this fixation of structure is in danger of missing freedom, creativity and goodness. But not only the natural scientist is in this danger, also the pragmatist is, who sees man as fenced in by the structure of an atomistic society of success, of cash-value. Teachers and physicians may make a common cause in subjecting life to a setting, which gives comfort, by arresting man in those routine functions which find appraisal and reward by society. In this way man will regard his endowment as a limiting factor, and he will think it quixotic and vain to attempt anything not predetermined by his nature. The careful man will anxiously avoid surpassing the limits traced by his potentials. The training of these potentials will be all that is wanted, in order that man may achieve an infallible and frictionless working of what will be akin to the animal-instinct.

The individual who is wrapped up in his nature, in his talents, is arrested in these very talents. Enjoyed as a possession such a talent becomes an obsession and possesses man rathers than that it is possessed. Pride and vanity will force him to exploit it in ever repeated routine which will ultimately arrest him in a barren scheme and destroy his talent. Only when the "nature" has become a unique springboard for a devotional life, talents, potentials will become fruitful and expand beyond their original limits. Even when nature has treated man in a niggardly way, the energy of a directed life, devoted to others, will carry to unexpected heights. Such a man may still cherish his "dispositions" as a possession, as a treasure, to be held together and augmented, for all education is just this, the training and widening of a ready possession, a content of consciousness. But man should not stop here. He should subject his nature, his trained possession to the service of a greater life, and transform it, in the dynamic and directed outreach beyond himself, to a unique springboard for his service. Thus it will happen that what had been a content and possession only, a material, becomes now an inspiring power, an indistinguishable element in the drive and outreach of person to person, and what had been a weight only, limiting and arresting man, will be a wing which carries forward and beyond. As such an inspiring power "nature" will not be limited and reduced to a specific structure, of body or character, it will embrace and include in its uniqueness of outreach all things, all bodies which are able to enter in and to serve the communion of love; all these things will become unique and will inspire as a springboard and a call the responsibe devotion to a communion which reaches out infinitely and will ask for an equally unlimited stimulus. We remember that even in the sphere of a mere potential vitalism body and things were not just "objects" in their environmental setting, but became also transparent, became indicators of motion and pointed beyond themselves to a power toward which man aspired, if only gropingly and in vain. Therefore it is evident, that here in the meeting of person with person the objective nature, the content of consciousness in its situational fixation, the character, conditioned by environment, will become not only transparent, opening up into empty Existence, but will reveal itself as part and parcel of that very force which lifts us beyond ourselves. We mentioned above that the free will does not receive its material as externally and accidentally given, but that it moulds its material as belonging to it, responsible for this material, for the "situation" which in its turn inspires the will. Thus all things in our reach become transmitters, become inspiring forces which keep us on the way toward fulfillment. The selfenclosure and estrangement of man melts away and he becomes an exponent of a wide and all-comprehensive desire, regarding all things, alive and lifeless, as his responsibility, widening the scope of his aspiration infinitely, although it still is the Thou of the beloved person which continues guiding him and providing a firm direction.

It may not be easy, however, to break the crust of one's own bodily seclusion and to look upon one's own character not merely as a disposition to be utilized for the development of the self but as an aspiration to reach infinitely out to other lives. But inasmuch as the communion of love gets hold of us and makes us indispensable to others, the more will we become aware that our possessions, our "Nature," our talents are not a mere material to be molded, but are in their turn inspirational forces, just as the nature of the beloved person is not something statically given, but a dynamic call, a demand and invitation to discover and to realize. In this way "matter" loses its meaning, matter as set over against form, structure as separated from process. The distinction between matter and form is here out of place, a mere reflective abstraction, ultimately foreign to the realm of reality. Both, form as well as matter, are forces which, in togetherness and cooperation enrich and even constitute each other. To be sure: Matter, seen from the perspective of form, appears as a principle of conservation, of inertia and fixation. But such a conservation and fixation is not "resistance," but rather concentration of energy. Seen, on the other hand, from the perspective of matter it may seem as if "form" had a destructive nature, although it is in fact by no means destructive, but, on the contrary, a fulfillment of the potentials, dormant in matter. Modern existentialists have emphasized the negating and destroying aspect of form, but they have perverted the truly creative and positive character of the formative power, with regard to which matter is a readiness to be converted and lifted by transformation to a higher status of being. There is, of course, an element of surrender and even of sacrifice, which with regard to the body may appear as "mortality"; but mortality is not destruction, as death would be, it is rather the condition for an ever new birth, clouded by the necessity of giving way, of frailty, and thus imbued with seriousness and responsibility.

Only in the living communion of forces is the rigid opposition of form here and matter there resolved: everything is as well form as matter, in need of the other and shaped by the other. Body not only, but beyond body environment; environment not only but beyond environment the whole wide World have here become opportunities for formation, a responsible readiness, even a call and inspiration for creative transformation. A "situation" is here nothing without the power which forms it. The "Kosmos" is, what body already dimly suggested in the realm of imagination, not only a ready setting but also an inspiration and call for an infinitely varied transformation, a present which guides toward future and demands this its future. In this way every thing, every event will be adored in its presence, but also as a springboard for the future. The World which in anxiety and hope had been approached from a distance and had withdrawn, denying itself to consciousness, enters now the lives of men and reminds them that the presence is meaningful only when it leads beyond itself. Nature which had dimly only responded, has become an inexhaustible source of inspiration, unique, wherever grasped, radiating faith and confidence.

What we call very inadequately a "Culture," as if it were a medium shaped by our arbitrary doings and adapted to our subjective moods, is this web of inspirational forces unfolding in a progressive sequence, beyond mere purpose, utility and possession. And here we may be reminded of the beginning of this chapter, when we first faced the problem of freedom and discovered it in History: History is the unfolding of Culture, carried by faith in an ideal, embodied in personality, realized in a communion of devotion, in which every fact, every event receives a new and unique meaning, a "physiognomy" of its own.

This cultural structure grows, perpetually deepened and intensified. Culture can be regarded as if it were an order, a medium, filled with things and events. But, unlike the medium of space-time, Culture does not only receive these things as given in its structure, not even as material and disposition to be formed. Culture creates new things and new events, new, because they are **one** in their inseparable unity of matter and form. Their "material being" is that power which calls for a meaningful unfolding; the situation is just this, that it is pregnant with a future and carries ahead. In this way the static and isolated closure, the estrangement and privacy of things, their "past" in its seeming fixity, abandons its dead and finished character and becomes the cradle of a living future. What we call "tradition" is such a past which as past and in spite of its somehow closed nature, opens up, not by subjecting the future and depriving it of its newness nor by meeting with the future in a static present, as this was done on the level of imagination,[8] but as a service and fertile ground for the future, imbuing the future with ever new life. It is in loyalty to the past, in faith rooted in tradition, that History shapes the future, and it is this paradox of a past pregnant with the future, of the old as the cradle of the new which is essential to Culture and History. Far from wavering between old and new, between conservatism and rebellion, a steady progress unfolds in loyalty to the past. There is danger, however, that man, weak in his faith, is unable to carry his past as alive into the future, but that he either roots himself stubbornly in the past alone or worships exclusively a future torn away from the past. In such a case History loses its character and degenerates either into a stagnant repetition of a dead past or into a rebellious experiment with a future which glorifies the new for the sake of its newness. While in the former case man surrenders to a hardened past with a semblance of humility which, however, is rather a lack of confidence and a craving for security, man in the latter case is driven by "hybris," by a faithless confidence in himself as the giver of ever new laws.

Only when man has understood the twofold truth which Culture reveals: the unity of a closed past and an open future, of that which lends itself to the forming power and this power itself in its unfolding, of tradition and progress, of a preserving ground and of a call for change, only then at last is he able to understand and answer the question which haunted him: how far and in what way may Reality truly enter our knowledge, which is after all only "knowledge about reality." [9] The answer will be this: Our abstract and scientific knowledge is a true knowledge and not a mere illusion because of the cooperation of a given Nature and of an organizing mind, both of them being elements of one and the same reality. The activity of knowing man, his organizing and abstracting procedure is only one of the integral factors of knowledge; the other is the factual and given element, which indeed would remain opaque and closed and foreign to man's endeavor, if it were a mere material, divorced from the organizing activity of man. But, in fact, man's activity and devotion is inspired by a nature which belongs to it, which not only lends itself to this activity, but calls for it, as its inherent and essential structure. In the first chapter of this our essay it was the organizing process of thought and of abstraction which devoted itself to a "fact" which as absolute and independent revealed itself in the sacrifice of a selfeffacing thinker. This selfeffacement was not an arbitrary act, but was dictated by factual reality as such, and it remained an essential facet of our knowledge, coming ever clearer into focus, that the split between knower and known was step by step more and more overcome, until the distance between an opaque world of existence and the lighted realm of man's consciousness disappeared in the mutual interaction and constitution of personalities in a communion where the estrangement between a matter which is lifeless and resisting, on the one hand, and a form which usurps all the credit of creativity, on the other, is ultimately wiped out. It is, therefore, true that we are opened to "forces," to "relations," and "substantial structures" most intensely in the experience of our communion with other lives; that we find "force" in the free personality, "substantial balance" in the structure which unites person with person, and that the abstract device of "relation," as a unity in spite of the plurality of its elements, becomes dynamic in the "communion of love" which is a unique, concrete, and living unity, constituted by separate but—in spite of their separation—profoundly integrated and united lives. Even "causality," that wasp-nest of paradoxes, which is closed in each of its stages and at the same time open: the cause closed but open to the effect and revealing in every part-condition the whole cause,—all this is experienced and made most meaningful in the living communion of personalities. For it is in the communion that the person is closed and unique, but open also in his uniqueness to others, and any fragmentary experience brings the "whole person" into play, opening him up to his neighbor. Finally the "symbolic representation" of the propositional realm, the standing of the symbol and its substituting for a wider truth, finds its ultimate confirmation in the "metaphorical representation," where each entity not only stands and substitutes, but enters into others in interaction, revealing in sacrifice and intercession the wider structure and unity of love.[10] We may regard the orders of Logic, of Mathematics, of causality and of conceptual intention as "analogies" to the order of reality, as revealed in communion and love; but these analogical orders do not find, as the Schoolmen thought, a "confused analogatum," a vague unity only (p. 15); on the contrary, the vagueness, the "confusion" or rather the inadequacy resides in the various abstract orders, in their reduction, their fragmentary perspective. All these reduced orders are insufficient with regard to reality; even the order of perception and imagination is still only a reduction, and thus our knowledge on this level is only "knowledge about reality." We understand now what this "knowledge about reality" means: it means an analogical perspective, true as far as it goes and surely a working device, but not a full insight into reality as such. When Kant regarded causality, substance and reciprocity in space and time as analogical, he was not altogether wrong; but he was wrong in placing the "analogatum" in a pure "category," instead of finding it in the purity of freedom, personality and communion. It is because of the insufficiency and merely analogical status of cause and substance that in the transitional phase of imagination these two categories, cause and substance, show their indefinite character in the face of existence and convey only a "probable necessity," which, however, points beyond itself to a free necessity, clarified and brought into focus as the communion of living and interacting forces. In this communion, at last, the abstract orders of scientific organization receive their ultimate justification.[11]

But a new danger presents itself here: The justification of order by an interplay of forces should by no means be interpreted in a utilitarian or positivistic way. It is not man's need and comfort and their satisfaction that make truth to be true and knowledge to be known. The anthropological fact "man" has to be embedded in a deeper layer of reality. We have not followed the long and weary road from simple abstract order, from time and space, from substance, causality and meaning to living duration and the surrender to World and Existence in order to get arrested in a mere usage of this World by the human animal with its skill and agility, exploiting the possibilities which its organs provide. To be sure: There is such an animal, but its skill has to surrender to powers which disclose its frailty and justify it only in so far as it reaches the status of a "person," and even here only in the devotion to a communion of service. In its isolation and singularity it is given over to death, is frail, mortal and without value, but receives value and meaning in the communion of its cultural setting. This communion becomes the person's destiny, a necessity which freely works and which involves him in decisions by which he participates in the freedom, ruling over his life. We may call this free necessity of destiny "divine"; but this remains a mere word, as long as we do not fill it with the meaning to which our long road of approach has opened up, a metaphysical ground and foundation, limiting as well as justifying man in awe and in faith and guiding him into actions.

This faith is a reality and it carries our life. But it is far from making this our life easy and far from providing us with a smooth directive for our doings. There is a paradox in this faith, a paradox which is akin to the numerous paradoxes we met on our way, and thus fundamental. Faith in its fullness is aware of a twofold and almost contradictory truth, resulting in contradictory attitudes: There is faith in the stability of our World, in a power of preservation; but in spite of this stable preservation the past is perpetually breaking away toward a future, which, inspired by the old, transforms it and in transforming destroys. Culture and History call upon man, not only to worship tradition and preserve it, but also to negate and reform. Man receives from Nature the inspiration which makes him say "Yes" to all its wonders, but also the call to tear himself away, to take leave and to abandon. This appeal to abandon, however, will not result in the alienation and separation, which characterized the imaginative longing for a distant and unknown World beyond. Man will not cease to regard the World as his own, as his responsibility, and he will continue to love what he has to challenge and to destroy.

He will not deny the defects and ugly facets of his World, hypostatizing it into a divine order of pantheistic contentment. Responsible for a future, he has to bring about, called to his task by the very World he has to challenge, man is driven with a sorrowful intensity toward a truth which he is destined to "make come true." In this prophetic task man will be inspired by a twofold freedom: He will be free in his adoration and preservation of the World's beauty, and he will be free for the tragic task of a destructive reform. This twofold freedom will echo an equally twofold vision of a guiding power beyond: An eternally present power of preservation, a haven of security and peace; but at the same time a call to the future, demanding sternly and sending man into the battle of his responsible action, where he risks security and the happiness which goes with it. But even this call to action and challenge will not force man into a hostile attitude toward that which he has to challenge, nor will it involve him in the dualism of a mythological ambivalence, good and evil inextricably united: There is neither "good" nor "evil" on this most fundamental level of reality, but merely the free necessity of destiny: to acknowledge the present beauty of a World which has perpetually to be sacrificed and transformed for the sake of an unknown future.

Throughout the ages man has pondered whether the divine power is immanent in its World or whether it transcends it. If immanence means identity of the Divine and the World, then the divine power is not immanent at all. But if we understand "immanence" to mean the eternal presence of the Divine which keeps the World alive, preserves it and gives it meaning, then indeed the Divine is immanent. But not only immanent: It transcends the World in so far as it detaches itself from its creation, turns toward it with a stern demand, with a call to the creatures which makes them responsible and allows them to reshape perpetually the divine creation according to their own free responsibility and decision. As immanent the divine power is approached in humble devotion and, although most near to man as the ground of his existence, it is worshipped in total dependence which makes man feel insignificant in the divine presence. In its transcendence, however, the Divine, although rising into lofty heights, calls man to its side, demands that he become creator in his turn, lifts him into divine nearness and asks him to transcend in his own small way, to transcend the security, comfort and joy of the World which remains as a foil only, a ground of support, lending courage to man, when in the face of agony and suffering he is called to sacrifice and destruction.

VII. SIN, GUILT, SACRIFICE AND LOVE

History has two faces. Its meaning is expressed in the stable structures of cultural fulfillment, satisfied in their unique achievement, preserved in the presence and immanence of an all-embracing power which makes all things into living things and into instruments of joy. Thus plays and pageants, houses and gardens, and even the daily customs of a living culture come to express the beauty of a balanced setting and give delight also to those who in a later age are confronted with that life, long ago buried and destroyed. But this delight has its dangers: It provides an easy satisfaction of solidarity, of a happy absorption in an all-unity, a weakening of personal responsibility. This absorption is undoubtedly an urge, deeply rooted in the human soul, especially in Eastern culture, a mystical longing to vanish in the All-life of a Divine Being. It is, therefore, a highly important aspect of history that its second face is turned away from this pantheistic contentment, that Western man has been rescued from this all-absorption and loss of individuality by a call toward the future, a demand which breaks into the peace of a cultural fulfillment and channels the powers of the individual in a transforming and partly destructive activity, disturbing and tragic, involving in suffering and death. Without this darker aspect history would miss its depth, and its phases would fade into a stagnant repetition, dull and without the unforgettable mark which is essential to it.

The call comes to the individual as a call to take responsibility, and it comes from another life, loved and adored, from a "Thou," with whom the individual is united in a unique and exclusive communion. But this unique communion is welded to the all-embracing unity of lives which the cultural setting had provided. It is the paradox of history, that its bearer is alone in his responsibility, alone exposed to the call and to the life from which the call comes, but that this very responsibility unites him with the destiny of all other lives in his reach, with all other lives for which he feels responsible. It is again the paradox of the urge of preservation, of oneness with the present and the solidarity of lives, on the one hand, and the contradicting urge to break away, to mould and change, but both urges unified in one and the same responsibility, which gives rise to the unique phenomenon of "Intercession": Historical man acts in intercession for an unlimited number of lives, with which he is one and which he seeks to protect, but which he has at the same time to divorce from their defences, their security, in order to lead them toward their future. Thus the historical man is a "representative" of his cultural group, but as representative singled out individually and responsibly in lonely isolation.

Man lives in the face and under the call as a "representative" of the frail lives around him. He represents these lives not in the static and abstract way, by which an instance represents a law or a particular "stands for" a general entity as a symbol of truth. He is not a representative of the "genus" man. Such a symbolic representation was hailed by Greek thinkers as the highest fulfillment of human destiny. The representation we are concerned with here is very different: It is a dynamic, a "metaphorical" representation, not a symbolical one, concrete, unique, responsible before another greater life and responsible for a multitude of concrete, individual lives which are in need of guidance, of being lifted out of the rot of their stagnant present situation. Representative, intercessional man has to risk in order to protect, has to hurt in order to heal: it is the tragedy of prophetic historical man that he is deeply aware of the frailty in all present contentment, that he anticipates and even brings about suffering and loss, while his people indulge in the satisfaction of the present and indignantly turn against the troublesome caller. This has always been and will always be the tragedy of the prophet, who feeling one with his people destroys his own happiness together with their's, suffers with them and is torn in the contradictory duties which rule his life.

What gives courage to the prophet in this tragic situation is the understanding of the deeper meaning in his conflict: this understanding will come to him as a "revelation" of guidance, as a vision with regard to the greater life from which his call came: He will understand that his conflict mirrors the twofold nature of the source of his call: there will be a disturbing and demanding power as well as a comforting and preserving strength, both united in one, as they are united in his own conflicting and tragic life. The power of all-unity and unchanging presence will come to him as a super-personal principle raised above all lives, although imbuing all lives with its quiet presence of love. But this very same superpersonal power will reveal itself also as a disturbing and dynamic force entering into the lives which it stirs up, taking its place in the communion, itself a person, a partner in the process, besides being the ground of all process,[1] reached by the human person in a personal relation of devotion and prayer. This twofold nature of the divine power is an expression of the complexity of reality as we faced it throughout this work; but it is also experienced in the history of the race where God was understood as well as an impersonal principle as "Law of Heaven," as "Tao," as Brahma Nirguna, as "Godhead," but at the same time also conceived as a personal God, as Brahma Saguna, near to his creatures, incarnated not in the flesh, but in the spirit, as a loving, compassionate and even suffering God, in a convenant with man, responding to man's needs and by responding changing with these needs.[2] Suffering assumed in this mature vision a positive and creative aspect. To shun suffering, instead of sharing it, meant now a turning away from ultimate reality, a loss of salvation.

To suffer and to inflict suffering is the tragic destiny of a loving and responsible life. Not only religious prophecy, but also tragic poetry places this insight into the center of its vision. Death is not simply a biological fact, it is meaningful when understood as "mortality," that is as readiness to be formed, to develop and to be exposed to suffering and destruction. We do not live "toward our death" as the rounding out and fulfillment of our life, as some existentialists want to make us believe; but we have indeed to build death and suffering into our life as a necessary element in the formation of the future. Life is a sacrament, a sacrificial readiness. "Sacrifice" has the complexity of destruction for the sake of preservation on a higher level. Thus the two conflicting urges are reconciled and the paradox resolved.

All lives, all actions, even all things and events are sacramental, when seen in this light. Biblical prophecy discovered the sacrament as the most adequate expression of religious devotion, and this expression should have replaced the "ritual" of former times. Rituals are "symbolic reductions," expedient devices to facilitate the understanding and managing of the divine abundance, devices to close the Infinite into the handy form of a finite structure. Such practical devices have their advantage, but also their danger: they substitute the finite for the infinite and thus, intending to open a path to God, they often conceal, instead, the intangible divine life within their tangible structure, cutting man off from its sharing. They tend to concentrate all holiness within the fences of their limited structure, and so they deprive all other things, outside of the ritual, of their inherent holiness. They may even pervert into mere magic, as a device to master the holy and to put it to use.[3] The sacrament, on the other hand, does not close the Divine into a finite pattern and does not try to master it; on the contrary, it gives finite things, even our finite lives away as an offering and opens a sphere beyond. Everything, therefore, not only those things which have been arbitrarily selected for ritualistic use, have to be regarded as sacramental and lead beyond their frail enclosure into infinity. St. Francis and Brother Lawrence knew that every humble action and object are holy and carry with them an element of prayer and redemption, a sacramental flavor.

But it will now be necessary to search deeper into the complexity of preservation and destruction, of the sacramental nature of man as the fundamental aspect of his life. The necessity to follow the call and to transform, hurt and destroy does not acquit man from his responsibility. It is a free decision in a free communion with the life from which the call came. When Greek mythology emphasized the tragedy of man as the suffering of an irresponsible victim, caused by a hostile fate, it had to be corrected by a maturer vision, foreshadowed already to some degree in Greek poetry. Here the inner unity between fate and man was discovered, his personal "destiny," which is the free response to the call, the decision of man to take upon himself the agony of destruction. He accepts his destiny as a free responsibility, and he confesses this responsibility as his "Sin."

Sin is a fundamental predicament of mature man, who obeys the call which came to him from a greater life and leads him into suffering, death and destruction, as a necessary preparation of a future for which he is responsible and which he has to bring about, not for his own sake, but for all those which he lovingly represents in intercession. Sin is, therefore, not really a violation of human life, although it involves the destruction and offense of human security; it is rather a violation of God's creation, a destruction of the presence and beauty of God's World. Sin is thus a religious status of man. But it is not a "revolt against God," as the Theology of the Church has unfortunately misunderstood it. Sin is neither a revolt against God nor is it "greed" or "pride," all of these vices being exceptions and by no means shared by every human being. Not everyone and at every time revolts against God or shows greed and pride. But Sin is in everyman, it is the universal predicament of human nature, as this was again and again rightly declared. What, indeed, sin means, is the necessary and inevitable destruction of the present, of a beauty, loved and shared, but doomed to destruction by man who is destined to work toward the future. Historical man, the man of action, the prophetic man, has to obey the call which drives him into the tragic battle in which those whom he wants to protect, whom he loves, will be hurt. Man will always hurt those who belong to his past, parents and friends; misunderstood by them he will go his lonely road, for it is the call which he has to follow. But it is essential for the destructive nature of "Sin" that it is at the same time a service to a call, and thus it is justified in the face of this call and its origin. Sin is open to "grace," and it is this paradox which has been omitted and perverted by classical theology. Sin and grace belong together, as destruction belongs to the creation of a future which responsible man has to realize. What is endangered by sin is rescued by grace, in a necesssary and inseparable unity of wounding and healing, of condemnation and salvation, of "God's wrath" and "God's mercy." In sin and in grace man is united with all mankind and is relieved from the loneliness of his initial responsibility and intercession.

If, however, man is arrested in his isolation and loneliness, in an aggressiveness which blinds him against everything but the necessity to lay into ruins what he loved, then the call to the future is darkened and drowned in the fervor of destruction for destruction's sake. In his despair such a man, whom we may call a "demonic person," will try to storm his own heaven, an empty heaven, born out of a merely negative freedom of destruction. Such demonic persons, like Faust, like Nietzsche, like some of the modern Existentialists will have cut sin off from grace, and their sin, grown to enormous dimensions, will fill them with an equally enormous pride, with a selfreliance, akin to self-deification. Here we may, indeed, speak of a "revolt against God," but now as an exceptional perversion of man, not as a universal predicament, and in this "revolt" God will still be present: still there will be a rest of true sin, dimly surviving in this demonic perversion. Therefore our compassion will try to mitigate the demonic despair, for we know that at any time a return to the truly religious sphere is possible and even inevitable: The demonic is after all only a perversion of true faith, as every passionate atheism is a disguised and perverted love of God.

But when man has totally divorced his ego from any communion of love and service, when he complacently and cynically idolizes his own will, then he has become "evil," and the evil man has lost his truly human nature. "Evil" is in contradistinction to "Sin" not a predicament of man, but rather a pathological state, an accident, an accidental "fall" from his human and divine nature. Theology has confused sin with evil, the fundamental human existence and the accidental fall. Thus theology had to take refuge to forces of evil, to the snake in paradise and to the devil, mythological inventions for the sake of explaining the exceptional perversion.[4] The philosopher, however, has to correct this error and to restore the inherent unity of sin and grace.

The awareness of sin opening up into grace constitutes the drama of "Conversion," a drama which is fundamental for the whole life of the religious man. This conversion will take place at a certain time and in a certain situation during the course of life. But once it has occurred, it never stops to influence and guide the future existence. Surely, Paul received his conversion on the road to Damascus. But from this moment on the drama of sin and grace gave its character to everything he did. Out of the night of the soul—so the mystics testify—the spark and flame of divine truth is perpetually reborn. We are in a state of perpetual conversion, never totally in the light nor ever totally lost in darkness and despair. We have, indeed, to act, to do and thus know ourselves as sinners, doomed to destroy and perhaps to die in this destruction. But this death, like all doings, has here the character of "tragedy," that is: in death and failure grace is revealed. Tragedy originated in Greece as a religious service, and wherever a tragic event strikes us, we are on religious ground. Man will, therefore say "Yes" to this tragic destiny and accept it. The mythical attitude to fate, resignation, has changed into a free sacrificial acceptance, a sacramental vision. Not only mythology, also magic and ritual have lost their meaning, for the ambivalence and insecurity of life which asked for protection, has vanished in a confidence, a faithful sharing and free abandonment, which is at the same time a free activity to bring about the truth in which man believes, and for which he is responsible. This sacramental attitude is foreshadowed in Greek tragedy, although the mythological origin keeps the hero in darkness and ignorance as an innocent and irresponsible victim, until he rises in indignation against the hostile mythical fate as well as in indignation against his own supposed innocence, and he now either asks for his punishment as a free and responsible sinner (Oedipus) or is lifted up to the level of the power from which his destiny came (Prometheus liberated).

It is, therefore, not a matter of chance that the great tragedies of Greece and of the Christian era, the tragedies of Aeschylos and Sophocles and the tragic masses, offering Christ's death and resurrection, were conceived and enacted in a service, in which the whole community took part. For these tragedies unfold man's unity in sin, sacrifice and intercession. It is the invisible Church, beyond any organization, which gave birth to these dramas as a "Cult," as an expression of the community. What welds the Church as a community, into one single body of worship is the awareness of mutual intercession, each member responsible for the life of all. Not comfort or security is the mainspring of common worship, but the unity of the call. It is the heightening of responsibility, the intensifying seriousness of the burden, not a lightening by sharing and dividing.

The organized Church has not always understood this heightened responsibility as the meaning of its existence, but has rather tried to reintroduce the mythical lifting of responsibility and the restoration of innocence. It has subjected its members to a law from above, a holy necessity, a dogmatic structure, manifested in a prescribed and repetitive activity of rituals. Systematization and ritualization have furnished an alibi for those who cannot live up to freedom and responsibility. The average man, weak and easily discouraged, has eagerly accepted the help which rationalization provided in a handy system. Certainly this help was not meant as an escape from responsibility, but rather as an aid to bear the burden of this responsibility. All systematization, including the scientific system, is a device to master an area, too vast and too problematic to live up to spontaneously and by immediate experience. Thus theological structures, as scientific ones, are meant as aids. But they have, indeed, in the course of history, served at times rather as devices of descent into easy security, instead of ascent to freedom, rather devices of escape from personal responsibility, where responsibility was asked for. This is the ambivalent character of most human endeavors, that they are born out of good will, but are apt to drag man downwards. It is futile to curse this human predicament, as if it was a gift of the devil. It is, on the contrary, a treasure to be grateful for, if used in the right spirit. When this is done, rationalization, dogma and ritual serve a sublime purpose, helping man on his strenuous road upwards. Weak man will abuse the gift of organization and will use dogma and ritual as means for security and a shelter against responsible freedom. This was what Dostoevsky tried to show in the sublime story of Christ before the Great-Inquisitor in the "Brothers Karamasov." It may indeed happen that the organization of dogma and ritual makes man to a mere passive executor of a clearly defined divine law and thus divorces him from freedom, from sin, but also from grace and faith. In its barrenness the lawful necessity will be stripped of the dynamic tension of sin and grace, and men will remain resigned in a mechanism of behavior which may still be called sinful, but which introduces a hardened lifeless concept of sin. And, instead of grace, this necessity will serve as a substitute, a Divine necessity of law and judgment. Divine law and judgment will either be so far removed from the human sphere which is the object of this judgment that, lacking any contact with it, this judgment may appear to many as a whim, accidental with regard to the lives which in turn are left to accident without any guidance. Or the Divine judgment will in a quasi-scientific way express a law, closely united with its instances, the deeds of men, which as mere facts are now structured by the necessity of the Divine law, necessitated themselves and without possibility of free decision. In both of these rationalizations man will be faced by a situation which can scarcely inspire him to sacrifice and intercession, exposed to Divine acts which are either of an inscrutable accidentality or carry with them an inevitable necessity of law, in the light of which neither punishments nor rewards have any meaning, man being forced into every one of his actions.

What has, however, made these rationalizations acceptable to man, and what both rationalizations have in common, is that they deprive man of his freedom and unburden him of his responsibility. It seems that no solution is inacceptable for weak man which enables him to live without the unbearable and terrifying call to work out his own salvation. But with the elimination of a free responsibility grace is lost and with it the beauty of religious faith, the sublime task of representing mankind and carrying it with its agonies and suffering toward the redemption in God.

These rationalizations are not really true, for they are not the full expression of religious reality; they omit even what is most precious in our faith. But neither are they arbitrary and totally false. They have their root in reality, as all abstraction has; they represent the human situation. It belongs to our deficient nature that we have to rationalize, and these rationalizations can have a positive value when they stimulate man to go beyond them; they may become a challenge and even lead to conversion. Out of dogmas and rituals prophets draw their incentive to rise against the petrification of religious vision. All prophets start in the tradition of dogmas, and their passionate revolution is heightened by the existence of the very dogmas which became the springboard of their revelation. As a springboard, not as a prison, theological dogmas belong as an essential feature to the religious life. They belong to our lawful nature, to be remade in the conversion by which grace is born out of sin. The church, as a guardian of stability and law, had to emphasize the importance of dogmas and rituals, and they are indeed fruitful when used as an opportunity to rise, guided by the unique experience of the heart. All dogmas have to be "interpreted," not by abstract teaching but by the concrete experience of faith. It is here sacrifice again which saves the faithful man from getting arrested in his dogmas. Just as he has to sacrifice the lawful necessity of his "nature" in conversion, so he has also to sacrifice, remake and sublimate the dogmatic support which his all-too-human nature induced him to adopt.

Sacrifice, conversion, and the new life which they create, are of fundamental importance. It is the sacramental expansion which changes the World for man, and changes man himself for man. The praying man, in his communion with God, sacrifices himself and receives himself back through God's grace. But as he does not stand before God alone but as a representative of all those for whom he is intercessionally responsible, he receives grace for all of these lives and he receives them back as holy vessels of grace. Thus man's prayer is answered in the sanctificition of those for whom he prayed. While he carried them to God, naked and needy, in agony and sin, he sees them now as Divine shrines and thus he sees his neighbor for the first time in a new light, holy, blessed, a bearer of infinite value, while before there was only deficiency and need. So his attitude to man is entirely changed. It is God's holiness which shines to him from human faces, and the communion into which he enters with man is a holy communion, blessing him as he has brought blessedness by his prayer. But what should not be forgotten is that man is holy to man in his very human deficiency, holy as a needy, dependent, failing life. This is the paradox of human love, so very different from Divine love: that man is holy to man because he is a sufferer, because he fails and is without roots. His love is, therefore, turned to these very deficiencies, to the needs, to the body, and his service is "Care." Care is the mark of man's love for man, and care is essentially concerned with the body, that is with the needs linked to human limitation, realizing this care in clothing, feeding, giving security, education and a home.

Body has been discussed on the level of life and potential appearance. But there body had a precarious status, not really present in our experience, not a part of perception or emotion, but rather used as instrument only to reach through it, in an immediate contact, to objects outside.[5] Here, however, in the communion of man and man and on the level of creative freedom, where nature has revealed its formative and inspirational power, the body assumes a positive role: not object and not instrument, not disposition or material, but a source of loving care. It is through care that the body with its needs becomes an essential element in the experience of love. Here man sees and is deeply concerned about the bodily status of those whom he loves, and it is through his own bodily situation, his property, his social position, that he is enabled to care for the beloved. It is the bodily seclusion, with its limits, its shyness, its impotence of expression, its frailty, through which loving man enters into his communion. The shell of estrangement becomes an open door; faces, gestures do not hide but reveal, and by this revelation man steps into the sanctuary of the other's soul. It is now the radiance or the sadness of these faces which determines his happiness or despair, and it is through his power of gesture and physiognomy that he is able to affect the joy or the suffering of his neighbour. There is a new atmosphere, a new medium in which loving man lives, a medium of faces which need to be lit up, of bodies which are tired and need to be supported. Without this medium man would be lost, for it gives him his place in the World.

But though the bodily situation is important and is the immediate object of care, the communion of love is not a bodily communion; it is a communion of personalities, spiritual in character, no less spiritual than the communion of man with God. The body as an object of care is enjoyed merely as a "sacramental" object; it is transcended and preserved in that paradoxical way in which sacrifice is concerned with its object in sublimating it. To be sure, the sacrificial care for the body has long since parted from the primitive and cruel rites by which the victim received care in preparing it for its actual annihilation as a holy offering to the Divine power. The prophetic revolution has changed the manner of sacrifice from annihilation to a care which preserves the life and makes it by loving tenderness into a vessel of Divine presence. Since this prophetic revolution, no love of man for man can discard the care for the body, for the needy, helpless, and deficient shell of human existence; but this body-care reaches meaningfully beyond its immediate object into the spiritual core of the communion. The body is "cared for," but the personality behind this body is "loved." The body-care is the bridge between person and person, and it may even happen that the care for the body will have to include risk and danger for it, exposing it for the sake of the person; man is apt to risk his body and that of his love for the preservation and enhancement of the values which the personality-communion discloses. Man, when weak, may get stuck in the body, feeling the demand to transcend it as an unfulfillable task, and then he may be "ashamed" of this his body and the body of his love: they seem to stand in the way rather than to be a bridge toward personality. In a milder form this frustration appears as "shyness," as an impotence to reach through the body into contact with other people. But in both cases, in shame as well as in shyness, it is not fear of the unfavorable judgment of outsiders which causes shame and shyness, as Spinoza thought; it is rather the opposite; the inability to open up to others, the fenced-inness in the shell of the body makes men ashamed of this body, which should be his vehicle for transcendence toward other lives, not his prison. It may be that children are easily ashamed and shy, because they dimly feel the wish to make themselves understood, but are too immature to do so, when faced with serious demands.

The body is of a very specific nature and importance. It is not just a thing among other things, nor is its meaning exhausted by the role it plays in the fleeting and contingent life of appearance and imagination, over against a strange and fateful existence. In care and through care the body itself receives existence, becomes an expression of this power of existence, fully real in the communion of personalities and their mutual care. It is not life nor organic structure nor purposiveness which raises bodies beyond the sphere of contingent things; it is loving care, as the medium of personal communion, by which bodies partake in existence and assert their place in reality. Bodies as instruments and as objects for care, for service in the material sphere, assume because of this service a heightened reality.

It is the birth of "Ethics," of ethical man, out of the cradle of religion that we have tried to make apparent in the preceding pages. Ethics is grounded in religious experience, but, though this is so, the concern of Ethics has to take the bodily needs of man into account. It is care for these needs, it is service for the weak and helpless. And so it is not accidental that the prophets have turned the attention of moral man toward the orphans, the widows, the sick and the poor. But behind this care looms sublime the love for the Divine person in man.

The exaltation of our human existence, as it is characteristic for Western culture, is not a romantic and sentimental perversion. It is a profound insight derived from a truth which Biblical religion disclosed. Through the communion of God and man, as person to person, man's status has changed. Man is holy for man or, as Spinoza puts it, man is a God for man. The holiness of man and of human love is essentially grounded in the intercession of prayer and is, in a way, the fulfillment of this prayer. The grace which man receives is his new insight into the holiness of those who are his responsibility and of his love for them. Love of God is, therefore, the ground out of which the love of the neighbour emerges. The one cannot exist without the other.[6] This divine kinship of our human love is, however, not diminished or soiled by the fact, that it is directed toward the body, and that care for the body fulfills much of our human love. Our love for our small children is fully absorbed by the bodily care which these helpless little creatures need; and it is only after they have grown that our care widens, transcends the body and is sublimated to a spiritual friendship which, in spite of the continuing body-care, will be directed to the sacrifice of merely bodily values. Our adult love will, however, return in old age again to the predominant care for the body, when we take care of our weak parents and friends. Care and the body are with us in all our human love and in all our moral relations, so much so that we miss bitterly this body-care, when death has taken our beloved from us, and when our love beyond the grave can find fulfillment only in a spiritual contact and communion. By the death of a beloved person the immense importance of bodily presence and care is revealed; how much it meant to us to kindle the light in the eyes of those whom we love and to protect them against sadness manifested in the tired gestures of their body; how we long to give radiance to those eyes and make them smile again. The surviving life is utterly lost, it has been deprived of its place in the World. For it is care and only care which gives to man his spiritual place, constituting in the realm of reality a new order, a new medium of space-time. The place which a man has as a personality is indeed given to him by his body, not because this body has a certain dimensional extension, but because this body is the center from which care reaches out to other bodies. The "here" in this medium of space is the body as the starting-point of care, the subject from which care reaches out. The "there," on the other hand, is the body of him who is the object of care. The relation between this "here" and this "there" is an objective and even a material relation, but the spatial distance in this relation is not measurable in yards and inches. It is determined by the intensity and effectiveness of care between the two. How little importance yards and inches have for the determination of this distance is seen in the fact that a physical separation may bring the loving persons closer together and make them more aware of their mutual care, while too great physical nearness may weaken the intensity of care because of a routine which takes the care for granted and so destroys its essential meaning. The Biblical concept of the "neighbor" is exactly this spiritual relation of spatial distance, constituted by our responsibility of care. Everybody is our neighbour as long as, and to the degree to which, he needs us, wherever he may live.

Death of the beloved deprives the survivor of this his place, and he will float in darkness and emptiness, if not a rest of care, for memory and the grave of the dear-one holds him firmly in his place. But the tragic loneliness of death will be mitigated by the hope for a new order of care, a new home in another World to come, where lover and beloved are reunited forever. In this way death will be the door to a heightened reality, not of knowledge, as Socrates believed, but of love and care and responsibility for each other, eternal and beyond the grave.

Heaven is brought down to earth, and human existence is sanctified by care. This provides the World with a new grace; but the abundance of this grace leaves finite man in a position more precarious than ever, and makes him just as aware of his inadequacy with regard to those whom he loves as the sinner was aware of his inadequacy with regard to God's call: Surrounded by infinite demands of love, he will be torn in a conflict of loyalties, every life holy to him, every demand unique and all-absorbing. For love asks for total devotion. Man cannot divide his loving service and hand it out in small parcels. He must, wherever love finds him, give himself without restraint. Thus man is torn, unable to fulfill what should be fulfilled, denying himself here, because he is wanted there, and disappointing there, for his service to other loyalties shuts him out. Care binds man to his bodily finitude, to his limited place, and so his inadequacy falls as a shadow upon his soul. Although he will try his utmost to respond to these infinite calls, the tragic knowledge will deepen that failure awaits him in the face of a love as inexhaustible and manifold as this.

In the religious realm no conflict of loyalties interferes, for there is only **one** loyalty, the loyalty to God, and although this loyalty asks for a strength absent in man, his sinful failing is mitigated by God's grace. There is no mitigation in the tragic conflict of human loyalties, no grace which gives consolation and redeems. The Divine grace has spent itself in changing our human nature, for the sake of redemption, into a vessel of holiness, into a center of loving response. In intercession before God the needy lives were enveloped by an aura of God's grace, God and His grace absorbing fully the vision of the praying man. But now man has to face these lives, they come toward him and hold up to him their needs, their demands and hopes. With these infinite demands and hopes man has to cope alone and he has to find a way by means which his human nature provides. He will have to compromise, to ponder and to weigh his cares against each other and he will have to find a balance of distribution, strange in a sphere where no half- or quarter-fulfillment should occur. It is the "Conscience" which in this way ponders, judges and limits "duties" in an intellectual attempt at reconciliation. But it is this conscience also which knows that it ultimately fails and that its judgment does not exonerate but rather condemns its own decision as a failure, which in the face of an unforfeitable demand of love assumes here again the character of responsibility. Conscience makes us doubly aware of our responsibility and with it of our "Guilt."

Guilt is not sin. They are alike in that they are inevitable, and in the fact that in spite of their necessity they do not eliminate but intensify the awareness of responsibility, the one before God, the other before man. But sin is a more fundamental state of existence than guilt: it has its root in the mere fact of our living in God's presence. Guilt, however, asks for more specific conditions: it depends upon a conflict of loyalties, not simply upon our communion with man. It is possible to think of a situation without any such conflict, f.i. if only **one** loyalty were present. This would surely be an exceptional case, but the fact that such an exception is imaginable makes guilt a less absolute and unavoidable element of life than sin. We attach guilt not so much to our human nature as such as to our actions, not so much to love itself as to the carrying out of love's demands in the sphere of bodily care. But, of course, bodily care is essentially united with our human love; and although all works are accidental when seen in the light of personality and communion, the care for bodily needs is not accidental but of a specific importance. In the conflict of loyalties the necessity of care is the factor which brings the conflict to the fore and forces us to sacrifice some of the demands. We may link our guilt, therefore, to specific actions of the past, to specific endeavours of care, and looking back we may "repent," as if our failures could have been avoided and as if we "have become guilty" in a certain moment of our past, dreaming of an innocence we have lost. But we know, in spite of this, that our guilt is not an accident but a necessity grounded in bodily limitation and care. It is the shadow which falls from action and care onto the free communion of personalities, not simply caused by the mechanical course of natural events, but by the conflict in care and thus in love itself. Man will again and again try to shake off guilt, he will not humbly take upon himself the destiny of his guilt, as the sinner carried his sin, resigned in God. He will revolt against his guilt, never reconciled to his situation.

But just here we grasp the nobility of man. His faith gives him courage to keep on fighting, although reason tells him that he cannot succeed. Guilt, like sin, has a positive, a creative power; it is not a purely negative element, not foreign to love and excluded, but included as a condition for our courage, for our striving, an indispensable intensification of love and freedom. This courage, though seemingly frustrated by guilt, is not a meaningless adventure, as some existentialists believe. The faith which underlies the struggle is the power of love itself and triumphs in the spirit, even if in the body man will be defeated. It is here that the "intention" of man's moral action separates itself from motives and purposes. The latter will represent the compromise which our conscience has undergone, the practical result of the judgment, held before us for the sake of action to be carried out. But this intellectual compromise is grounded in a dynamic and uncompromising "intention" which is not reducible to a fixed practical purpose and which is often hidden from us, and surely hidden from the indifferent observer who sees only the limited purpose. The intention lives as a "general attitude," as a continuous direction of willing beyond the single purposes, motives, and their discontinuous decisions. Purposes are conceptual reductions of our wider intention, they are dictated by the environment and represent the compromise which the situation forces upon man. And these reductions will in their turn narrow down the dynamic intention to a mere "motive" which corresponding to the purpose will be a "motive for" the definite purpose, determined and determining, never free. It will under the pressure of circumstances be whipped up to a passionate desire and carry man astray. Man would, indeed, be lost in motives and purposes, if he had not infinite resources of restoration in the infinite direction of his willing intention, the full expression of his personality, not bogged down by compromise, but freely proceeding in the communion of his love. This unbroken continuous intention takes the reduced and blinded motives and purposes back into the stream of the will, raising ever-new attempts for carrying out its infinite demands. We may call the continuous intention the "intention of service," a service ready for sacrifice, rich in conflict and at times weighed down by the knowledge of guilt and failure, but always courageously facing its future. This intention, never exhaustively explained by motives and purposes, is a "way of life," and it was the wisdom of the Bible to emphasize beyond works and purposes, this "way," the way of the Saint, the way before God.[7] "I am the way, the truth and the life," are Jesus' sublime words, profoundly understanding the fundamental importance of the infinite intention which is an intention of faith and love. Faith beyond works, is what St. Paul preaches, faith as intention, as the "way," giving rise to works but never fulfilled by works. These works, when carried out in human relations, are the necessary reductions which conflicts of loyalty force upon man, his "duties" as compromises, laid down by the judgment of our conscience. Duties hypostatized by Kant to the essence of ethics, to "the Good" as such, are the expression of man's resignation in the face of conflict, a resignation which the intellect renders subtle, by giving it the structure of a system, the structure of "moral law," so that it can be carried out as a balance of duties. These duties will indeed, as Kant emphasized, ask for the sacrifice of "inclinations," but these inclinations are superior not inferior to duty; they are the loyalties which have to be suppressed because of the tragic conflict man lives in. The sacrifice of inclination leaves man, therefore, in a state of sad resignation and keeps his awareness of guilt alive, forced as he is to destroy values, like the sinner was; and thus the satisfaction which the fulfillment of his duty provides cannot compensate for the necessary abandonment of these destroyed and irreplaceable values. So the awareness of guilt is not eliminated but intensified by the tragic fulfillment of duty. A truly ethical man will not, therefore, be happy because of the fulfillment of his duties, he will want to do more, he will try the impossible and ask to remain true to each one of his conflicting loyalties.

In coping with mere things, with material possessions, man will adopt an attitude to these things which takes account of their accidental nature, when seen in the light of personality-communion and love. He will not make more of them than they deserve: he will "risk" them. Conflicts which present themselves on this level are not tragic; man will easily risk wealth, comfort and security when his loyalty demands it, and such risks will often be necessary in order to remain true to one's love. But in the conflict of love with love, manifested in the conflict of care, no risk is allowed; the gambler's attitude does not fit into the realm of personality and love. Here sacrifice, decided by conscience, not risk, is demanded, and here man has in resignation to carry out the judgment of his duty. Such a duty will, as the result of an intellectual weighing, be typical not unique, and so rational systematization enters the life of ethical man. And here we may once more touch on the problem of choice. In the conflict of loyalties, indeed, a balancing of alternatives must be acknowledged; it imposes itself on man, not as a symptom of his freedom, however, but as a symptom rather of his limitation, of his partial unfreedom, of conflict which makes him hesitate, ponder, weigh in his conscience between his duties and at last decide. This decision will presuppose indeed a choice between alternatives, it will have to rise out of a rational choice, but even here the spotaneity of love and its responsibility will ultimately be the decisive factor and will regard its choice and weighing of alternatives as a shadow upon its freedom, leaving man in the grip of his guilt.

Rationalization, having once entered and taken hold of ethical man, will try to usurp the field and will change what had been a symptom of limitation into a virtue and power.

Beyond the rationalization which conscience permits, a system of balance will be constructed with the aim of replacing conscience, responsibility, and all the conflicts resulting from the spontaneity of love. Man will want to shake off all the burdens of his ethical situation, and thus he will adopt a law-system of compromise which will provide the means for fulfilling all his duties, prescribed by the law. With guilt and responsibility thus removed man will feel secure. He will carefully fulfill every rule with a good conscience, even with pride. He will be one of those "righteous" who according to the Bible are less pleasing than one repentant sinner. He will be "perfect."

But this perfection and the security it provides are paid for by a loss of freedom. Law is raised above Will and determines it. Ethical systems as abstract orders replace the communion of love. We met a similar rationalization in the religious field, where dogma and ritual appeased the tension of sin and grace. But here the rationalization is far more dangerous because unrestricted. Theology may replace grace by Divine justice and subject man to the balance of law, but grace still breaks in, as "Divine mercy," singling out the individual and emphasizing the concrete communion with God. But in the abstract system of ethical law individual responsibility is entirely replaced by subjection to an abstract scheme, and conflict, sacrifice and risk, the pillars of a free and responsible decision, are eliminated. It is precisely for the sake of this elimination and the erection of a bulwark of security that the scheme of abstract law is here introduced. Responsibility and freedom have deliberately been put out of the way. Conscience and the awareness of guilt have gone too, have been replaced by a complacent sense of security. Man, protected in his actions by the command of law, knows himself justified, if he simply submits to its power. These systems are therefore not only outside of the realm of ethics: they are even destructive of ethics, walls erected against responsibility and freedom. The religious prophet may fight against dogmas, but he will rise out of the tradition which these dogmas present; they stimulate him, and he may preserve some of them when transformed by a new meaning. The ethical reformer, however, is not stimulated by the law-scheme he fights; he has to rely on his conscience alone.

Rationalists have tried to prove God and even to define Him. But these attempts were accompanied by doubt and by the confession that ultimately God was known to the believer only and only in the vision and communion of a religious life.[8] But the moral rationalist has eagerly gone ahead, defining and proving the Good. The Good was identified with the system of law, either with a specific positive law-system, the law of the country, or with the general idea of law as such, a timeless "natural law." The unsatisfactory character of these definitions, however, has made it clear that no true definition of the "good" can be given. The good cannot be conceptualized; it is no abstraction and it should not be used as a predication, although this is what we often do. A predicate is a perspective thrown on a thing in relation to other perspectives. But the goodness of a person is not a perspective, not a partial understanding of the subject; it is the expression of its full and inexhaustible being. It means the reality of the person, and it points to that which makes the person what he is: the communion of love. "Good" is only the personality in its creative freedom, and Kant was not altogether wrong when he cried: "Nothing is good in itself but a good Will."

Reality broke into the sphere of potential life in its phases of appearance and imagination as the miracle of "Existence," ineffable and absolute. This reality of Existence has found its elucidation in the realm of personality. It is the existence of communion between persons, the reality of love. This Existence, however, does not break in from above, but reveals itself as the innermost core of life, its value and meaning. Goodness is our word for this absolute Existence in man, while "holiness" would be the appropriate term for the Divine Existence. We may speak, however, also of God's goodness, as the source of all human goodness, communion and love. Absolute Existence, whether as goodness or as holiness, is not analyzable into single qualities or "essences." The medieval thinkers knew that God's goodness and His Existence cannot be caught in any essence or predication. It was the abundance of His Will, personality and love. But also in the human sphere goodness, as the absolute existence of the person, is not thinkable as predicate and cannot be subjected to the relative business of proving. The absolute never can. But besides this absolute Existence we may recognize a "relative Existence," the existence of location in space and time; [9] and similarly we may recognize besides the absolute good, a "good for something," that is a "usefulness;" and we may know besides absolute truth a relative truth, a truth in a context of a relational system. All these relativities are to be distinguished from their absolute counterpart, from absolute Existence, Goodness and Truth which surpass the conceptual realm of relativity.

Only the personality in its communion is absolutely good. If we call things or works good, we mean that they express or point to the goodness of a person.[10] This goodness of things is just as indefinable as the goodness of the person to which the good thing or work points and in the service of which the thing or work had been done. Service is a central idea in ethics; it is the bond which ties things or works to the ground of reality, the communion of personalities. Things are "existent" insofar as, in serving love, they are sacramental, and as sacramental they are not possessed, not "had," but are an expression of "being." Being, not having is the concern of love. Certainly the Will, struggling and entangled in the net of things, has to cope with them and may become endangered by acquisition and possessiveness. The Will is darkened by passion and threatened by possessiveness when on its road of liberation. It may happen that in order not to be possessed by things, the Will attempts to possess in its turn. But this attempt is doomed to fail, for possession is a form of being possessed. Possessions have to be risked in the service of love and only when risked do they lose their hold upon man. Also our possession of talents has to be sacrificed in a service of devotion, in order that they become the sacramental expressions of the goodness which they serve in the loving communion with others. In this way our natural gifts, which chain us to the world of success and glamour, and whatever other qualities we are proud of, receive a new meaning and protect us from being swallowed up by and arrested in our material achievements. Therefore love is not "motivated" by any talent or other glamorous quality in the beloved person: we do not really love a person because this person is intelligent or skillful or otherwise gifted, not because of these "possessions," but because of the fullness of his being to which these qualities and an infinite number of others are subjected, none of them standing out as important in its own right. Only those who do not love are attracted by specific qualities and rely solely on them, because they are not aware of anything but the observable facts. The loving person, however, does not so much observe facts, but shares the living person in his fullness, shares the goodness beyond definable qualities or gifts. Such qualities will appear in the course of the loving service and sharing, but then not as a fixed possession but as stages of an unfolding process for which love itself is responsible, discovering them and bringing them to birth.

Love is directed to a future, contained in the present. To be determined, motivated by fixed qualities or things means "infatuation," not love which brings freely into existence what is good in the beloved person, makes it "come true," responsible for the beloved in its faith. It is because of this dynamic creativity that faults in those whom we love are not obstacles but tasks, stimulating the intensity of our service and the awareness of our responsibility. Christ's attitude to the sinner should have taught this long ago, if teaching were enough.

The question is not: what or whom we love, but how we love, how intensively and sincerely. For such a love and its faith can move mountains. No human life is excluded from this love because of its deficiencies. Our love should embrace all lives in our reach, and it is only our bodily seclusion that restricts the scope of our loving service. In such a service no infatuation, no arrest in glamourous possession has room. It will be rather the failure, the deficiency, the weakness and suffering which open the heart for its service of love. Compassion will be a strong bond in the ethical communion of men.

We may "like" an object for its qualities, but we "love" a life for its inspiration, for the tasks it holds for us, for that which a loving service can discover and unfold in the future; and such an unfolding is possible in every person, when exposed to true love. And thus not the achievements, which the loving service may obtain, are the essential meaning of this service; it is the unfolding process itself in its mutual interaction and response. This meaning lies therefore not in the future, but is perpetually present in the stillness and fulfillment which the communion as such provides. In the face of this stillness all activity may sink into silence. But this silencing of Will and activity is misunderstood when it is turned into an ascetic renunciation of life wherein death appears as the ultimate fulfillment of love. The legend of Tristan and Iseult and other romantic novels of this kind have glorified total sacrifice as an end in itself, and this may have been done under the influence of Eastern mystery-cults.[11] But sacrifice should not eliminate, but preserve and heighten its object. Life may be sacrificed but at the same time sublimated, sanctified as a sacrament, expressed by the loving community as its goodness and meaning. It is not "Nothingness" but rather the fullness of Being which emerges out of the struggle of the Will with its guilt, a struggle in which the Will is lifted into a loving communion as an arc of stillness, an "amare in Deo."

The romantic hypostasis of death has been adopted by Freud who believed in a fundamental urge for death, confounding the urge for sacrifice with the urge for total annihilation and misinterpreting the positive character of sacrifice which is not directed to annihilation but to creation of value and to devotion. Sacrifice is carried by faith, and faith is faith in a life of love and communion. Not sacrifice should be turned into death, but death should be understood as sacrifice, leading beyond into a higher meaning. In this way death is indeed to be found in every deed done, in every act fulfilled, in every finishing off and taking leave. But all these deeds and acts which carry death point beyond their limited meaning and are never an ultimate termination, but are infinitely renewed. Unless we are arrested and get stuck on our way, these deeds are springboards only for further aspiration. Thus the Will in its struggle may be exposed to a hundredfold death, but personality and love rescue the Will and restore its power, lifting us into the higher sphere of an unending, ever-continuing service. In this way love proves stronger than death and the passing things we have to bury.

VIII. VALUE AND CREATION

The course of civilization has been shaped by two predominant attitudes: discovery and invention. They alternate and are sometimes closely connected. But their intention is different and so is the genius of those who are devoted to the one or the other. Discovery is a humble attitude, satisfied with approaching reality as an objective and independent power; invention, however, is exacting, imposing its subjective demands upon reality, and thus purposively transforming it. Primitive man was an inventor: his burning needs pressed him to invent protecting schemes for his security; the Unknown loomed before him as a threat and his attitude to it was fear. It is the same Unknown, however, which attracts the discoverer, his attitude is faith and devotion, and patiently he assembles knowledge as a service to a reality which fills him not with fear but with confidence. In unstable times discovery will be absorbed by invention and will serve as a means for an inventive protection. But if this happens, the result will be ambivalent: the technique and knowledge born of fear will bear more fear and will, besides protecting, endanger and turn against its own progenitor.

If this is so, then a full and truly justified attitude to reality will carry with it discovery as well as invention, both in an inseparable unity, without subjecting the one to the other. Here an active and dynamic process will be at work, moulding its objective as if this were a pure invention, but at the same time laying free in gentle discovery what had been present from time immemorial. We call this discovery which brings into being the very reality it discovered and makes it existent a "Creation." Creation has been a mystery since Biblical times. It was not fully recognized in ancient civilization, where knowing and making, discovery and invention, were neatly separated and where man approached an external World only, and this either by knowledge as unchanging or by action as mouldable, but always from outside. Creation became a vital problem only after man had turned from the external World to his internal life and had found here a reality, a truth which he had himself to bring into existence and which, in spite of being real, depended upon his action and was his responsibilty. Here the truth had to be made "come true" by the free working of the doer. We touched upon this paradox with regard to History and Progress.

Theology has coped with the problem of Creation. God's Creation seemed to be incomprehensible, if not proceeding in time, bringing forth the "New" in the way invention does; but it also defied time and change and disclosed the Eternal as only discovery does. What was dimly recognized was that Creation is essentially both: an invention in time and a discovery of the eternal beyond time.

The schism between discovery and invention has its parallel in the equally problematic separation of form and matter, overcome in the concept of Creation. Discovery emphasizes the unchanging form as a necessary structure, abstracted from a changing material of various possibilities. Invention, on the other hand, seems to unfold in a temporary activity conditioned by the necessity of a material upon which it imposes its ever possible forms. But after it has once and for all been understood that on the crest of reality discovery is invention and invention is discovery, this difference between form and matter, necessity and possibility, is discarded: Now Creation has transcended matter and form in a unity which is neither the one nor the other, but a living structure, and necessity and possibility have vanished in a unity which is called "Freedom." If we still want to distinguish between the two then we must concede that form is discovered as necessary, but also invented as possible, and equally that matter serves as a necessity, limiting the creator, but that it is at the same an inspiration, a possibility which unfolds and grows in the process of creation. To play out form against matter, the dynamic process of invention against the discovery of the stable Given, has, indeed, been the sin of Western philosophy and theology.[1]

To conclude: We are allowed to speak of Creation only, when the making is in fact the discovery of a Given, and when the discovery of the Given proceeds in its very making, that is, when process and structure are so closely united and mutually constitutive that they have to be regarded as one, so that none can be had without the other. The prototype of this unity and mutual constitution of process and structure is to be found in the unity of "personal communion" and of "value."

We may distinguish between Persons and value, but only by a reflective analysis. In reality they are one, and they are one, because they are a "Creation," the unity between inventive process and discovered structure. When we emphasize the processual and inventive element, we may speak of persons in communion; when we are concerned about the structure discovered in its unchanging sublimity, we become aware of "Value." Personality is in its structure

"Value," and Value is in its dynamic and processual character "Personality," both, however, in their unity a "Creation." The three mysteries: Personality, Value and Creation, opaque and hidden, when separately approached, lighten up when seen in their unity and mutual constitution.

Value is objective, a structure, and thus may seem to resemble law, order and fact. But it should be remembered that law, order and fact are abstractions, while value is concrete, absolute and unique. The question whether value is grounded in fact is awkwardly put: value is itself a unique fact, grounded in personality-communion; but personalities, in their turn, are grounded in value which they discover by their creative living. They are mutually grounded in each other, because they are ultimately one and the same, as process and as structure.

What has caused philosophers to retain the distinction and separation between person and value, is the fact that the structure of value seems to be raised above the persons as the law which rules over their communion, in order to be fulfilled by their way of life. But, on the other hand, the value-structure is just as much dependent upon the persons who discover it by their action, unfolding its lawful nature by their very aspiration. Thus the persons can be understood as sources and constitutive forces of value, but at the same time the value has to be recognized as the absolute guide and meaning of the communion, by which the persons find their tasks and fulfill these tasks.[2]

Here the problem of the "One and the Many" pushes to the fore, as it did in Religion and Ethics, and here, just as in the other realms, the problem centers around the enigmatic idea of the "Unique." Each person as well as the communion between them, is unique and absolute, and so is the value-structure, in spite of their plurality and relativity with regard to each other. Thus it may seem as if there were as many values as there are personalities, and in a way there are: but in spite of this the personalities and their values are absolute, wherever found, and universal in their validity.

This may become clearer when we now put a name to this unique character of value in its personal, dynamic, processual aspect as well as in its eternal stability and givenness: the word for it is "Love." Love is the reality in personality and beyond personality, created in the course of life and at the same time raised above this life as its guiding light, created, therefore, as well as creating. Love is not merely a subjective attitude, it is also an objective truth, a stable structure of unity. Besides being an "existential" power it is also an "essential" truth, revealed and discovered by those who humbly and devotedly grope for it. Existence and Essence, set over against each other in the sphere of struggle and appearance, are here united into one. This identity of essence and existence was recognized by medieval thinkers with regard to God, but it is true also with regard to human personality and human love, reaching toward and grounded in the Divine.

Love gives stability and ruling power to the person and at the same time breaks the shell of self-seclusion for the sake of a wider setting. What Plato saw was only the longing tension in the person, reaching beyond himself for something greater, and thus he denied love to the Divinity. But we understand today love in all its complexity, as a longing for a beyond and as a fulfillment of this beyond, as an awareness of an independent value, but also as the process which realizes this very value by its creative activity. And we understand that both these aspects are ever present and inseparable, the humble longing and the joy of fulfillment. Even the Bible has not rigidly separated the one aspect from the other, although God was predominantly the grace of fulfillment and man the seat of longing and hope. But, on the other hand, God reaches out longingly to man, and man's love is not without the power of fulfillment. Here we may be reminded of the twofold nature of the living "Force," its inward centeredness and its outward flow, close and open, stable in itself and manifested in its spending. Reality is always both, and so are personality and love. It was the error of early Indian thought to limit the Divine to a selfcontained, unmanifested life, degrading the World to a nebulous quasi-reality; and it was an equally disastrous mistake of Western man, to rely on the outward manifestation, observable and stable in relational terms, to such a degree that the creative force, responsible for the outward scheme dwindled away, leaving reality as a shadow of abstraction.

No wonder that in this scheme of abstraction value and creation lost their true meaning: value became a mere purpose and creation a mere purposive action. And, indeed, value is reduced to purpose and finds its realization in finite, relative things, in spatial and temporal action. But such things will never do full justice to the value they embody, for the value is infinite, unique and absolute, the purpose only finite, relative and abstract. Love in its abundance of value cannot be fully embodied in things or works. Even when things or works are done under the guidance of love, they are not "created," but only "made" or "done." A creation, a "creature" lives the full power of value and love, but things or works are subjected to the abstract law of causation or finality.[3] We had to reject the idea of creation, when faced by the mysterious but distant power of "Existence," never entering our fleeting lives, which remained in the distance of a longing only. A creation is, however, then experienced, when we are able to enter fully into it, for this is the way we understand it, not by knowing its purpose, but by sharing its creative process of existence.

Ancient culture only dimly recognized such living creation: even Plato's demiourgos remained aloof to his work and placed his creatures merely into a comprehensive pattern of order, where they found their meaning, but there was no entering into them and no holding them up into the light of love.

Only living beings can be regarded as "created," and only then when love had been at work. The non-living things, especially man's works and deeds are only "made," purposely and abstractly. If made under the guidance of love, then they may, besides fitting into a pattern of law, also point to this love, point to the personality, and thus carry a specific value, limited, however, and "instrumental" only, because they express the infinite value of personality and love in a finite way, in a finite perspective. We may call such works "good works," because they point to the goodness as the value of personality. Good works are only "somehow" good, never absolutely and wholly good as the loving person is. It was therefore a truth which Protestantism emphasized, that absolute values can only be lived in faith, and that all works remain inferior to faith. But Catholics were also justified in stressing that faith when strong will manifest itself in works, as inferior as they may be. When we regard the reaching out of the loving persons to others as a manifestation of love and faith,—although a manifestation which is one with its source—then the manifestation of love in works is only an expansion of this outreach, then the living communion, which alone can be called a creation and absolutely good, finds its expression in the abstract and purposive sphere of "good works." Love, however, does not necessitate these works with causal rigidity, as they belong to a lower sphere; love has not the necessity, which an astract law has with regard to its instances. The works, even when guided by love, are independent and subjected only to the order among things. As "instrumental" values they can never fully be explained by the love which guided them, and they will never express the abundance of value and love, they will not be lifted into the realm of this reality, but will remain in their own sphere, the sphere of things among things, of purposes and means, relative, practical, efficient or inefficient. This is the curse with regard to works, that their predominantly practical, efficient and useful character pushes to the front and suppresses the delicate and intangible element of value. Thus, proud of success, we regard the work done in its usefulness as the main meaning of life, while the love, the inner devotion, receive importance only as a kind of steam which has driven the human engine, so that production was done in abundance. This utilitarian attitude has vitiated our civilization and is a misplacement of value. The food given to the poor, the medicine given to the sick is all that counts; but neither food nor medicine as such are good, they are neither good nor bad; what alone is good, is the love expressed in this giving, raising love in those who received. Abstraction has confounded purpose with intrinsic value, and means with instrumental values. The old question, whether "ends justify the means" has its origin in this confusion. Means are neither justified nor condemned by ends, they are in a relation of practicality to each other; they are useful or useless, and this is all. But things may, apart from their usefulness, become an expression of value. In this case they receive a new meaning and may be regarded as "justified." Whether or not the burning of heretics was a means for salvation and practical for this end, may be doubted, and it was audacious of the Inquisition to be so sure of its practicality. But if this burning was the expression of true love—which it in fact scarcely ever was—then it was a valuable action. The physician who gives to the hopelessly suffering patient a strong dose of morphine and kills him does not use a bad means for a good purpose, but manifests his loving compassion, and hence his act is valuable.

Anything can become an instrumental value, sickness and crime, failure and grief. As mere facts they are harmful, but as manifestations of a loving service they may acquire a meaning which gives them value and justifies them. How often have loss and affliction intensified a loving life. But they could never be regarded and used as means for a purpose.

Value is not purpose. Kant's ethical command, to treat a person not only as a means, but also as "an end in itself" is an awkward statement and needs correction. No "end" is an "end in itself." What Kant meant, was not "end" but "value." The history of human culture advances beyond mere purposes and means into which pragmatism tries to close it. Animals may be utilitarians and pragmatists, but human religion, ethics and art are not of this kind. We seek God not for the sake of utility and comfort, we adore great works of art not because they give pleasure and entertainment, and protect us against boredom. We do not love and strive for truth for any advantage to be derived from love and truth. How far things, means and purposes, are from fulfilling the sphere of value is seen in the fact that often the sacrifice or at least the risk of such utilities is the way by which material things serve as instrumental values. "Nature" when understood as a World of things, of means, and of ends, does not fulfill value, and value cannot so much be found in this kind of Nature, as that by being sacrificed, by being transcended, this Nature may reveal a value beyond its own sphere. Nature in its abstract limitation is a mere disposition for the realization of values which are not just "natural" in this sense. Life is never such a Nature, although the degrees of creativity are various: there may be life with very little transforming power, rather fixed in its structure and embedded in the necessity of things. Our "character" is such a Nature, stable in its natural setting which as environment perpetually conditions the character. But even the character lends itself, in spite of its natural fixation and conditioning, to the creative transformation by personality, by that dynamic reality of value which rises beyond character, as its springboard for the working of love and service. Character may be regarded as an "instrumental" value, expressing the abundance of personality in a limited frame only, and we call such a character "good," just as we call a work, a deed "good": it expresses to a certain degree some facets of the absolute value of goodness, of personality and love. In the course of our life, fenced in, as we are, by character, environment, things and possessiveness, value in its absoluteness comes to us as an ingression from another World, and never will the data, abstract and detached and fragmentary as they are and as they open up to this ingression, explain in an adequate way, why this value entered our life. These data are, taken as such, a mere situation, beyond which, transforming and transcending it, value rose. We may be able to link the character and its actions to the environment and thus analyze them, but we are at a loss when asked to analyze and define the "goodness" experienced in a character and its deeds; we can only point to the love of the person, guiding the character in its fixation.

We are citizens of two Worlds: we are active, full of purpose, practical and bent to accomplish things in time and space, in an environment which is ours, our Nature and possession. But besides all this we are members of a communion of love, where no things, no accomplishments, no possessions as such count, but where works and achievements manifest our loving communion and nothing else. While in the material World everything is a want, a need, a pressure, but at the same time provides satisfaction in fulfilling a purpose, the World of value does not emphasize these short pleasures of an accomplished end. What is here provided is not pleasure, but happiness as a lasting state of free creativity, free from the pressure of things, but also free and open for love and communion as the sole realm where Creation has its full meaning. Unhappiness comes to those who know only of material things and the pleasure of possession. It is blindness to value, arrest in the pseudo-real sphere of material realizations, which makes man despair.

The relation between things and value, as considered in the preceding pages is a loose one; things belong first of all into their natural context, and their meaning is here determined either by mechanical causation or, if made as works are made, by purpose. As instrumental values they point to another sphere to which they do not really belong and which they disclose only in a certain perspective and in a fragmentary way. A "good work" is good merely in a certain perspective; it may not be good, when looked at from a different angle.

But there are some very specific works which are valuable in every regard, absolutely valuable, and which have their meaning exclusively through this their value. That they are purposively made is unessential, for their reality is only in the realm of value, nowhere else. These works are called "Works of Art." It is because of this that we speak of them not as "made," but as "created," and like all creations, they refute any merely inventional device, but are at least as much discoveries, revelations of value. They bring this value into existence as unprecedented, incomparable and unique. They are, of course, also made, and in so far invented and produced. But even this inventive procedure has the supertemporal character of the discovered, and it is therefore not consummated in a fixed result, but maintains its processual dynamism: Thus it is necessary to enter into this process in order to understand the creation. We understand the work of art not by knowing its purpose, but by entering into the process of its unfolding, sharing in this process as we share in the life-process of a person we love. All throughout our life we are surrounded by things which are what they are quite independent of the process which gave them their being, but the more dependent on other things for which they are useful, and it is this relation of usefulness which confers upon them the minimum of reality which they have. We may link these things to the realm of personal communion, but the meaning they thus receive is foreign to them; ultimately they remain strangers in the realm of ethics. We may go further and regard them as manifestations of a Divine creation, and then, indeed, they assume a reality which is absolute, a true "existence." But without this religious perspective they can scarcely be called "existent" at all, because what they are relies on their relation to something else, on their usefulness. But when we are faced with a work of art, the situation is very different: in a way the art-work is less independent, for it is what it is only as an expression of personality and is real only because of the value which we recognize in it; but it receives from this value indeed an absolute reality, a true "existence" which protects it from being swallowed up by other things and swallowed up by a shallow usefulness, relative to changing needs, to changing purposes and means.

How it is possible for an object in space and time, made to purpose, to preserve and express the creative process, is a mystery. What we can say in order to clarify the issue, is that wherever value is—that is, wherever a structure includes the process of its creation and therefore is alive—personality, communion, and love are on play. It may seem a mere analogy to speak of love as the meaning of art. But it is by no means meant as an analogy, just as in ethics and religion love is not introduced in an analogical sense. It would, on the contrary, seem strange, if art, one of the three great realms of spiritual realization, were excluded from that absolute value which governs the other realms. Therefore it is not at all far-fetched to regard the expression of personality and communion as the value and meaning in art; and as personality in its communion is structure and process at once, so also will the work of art necessarily and essentially convey the unity of process and structure and will because of that be alive. What deepens however, the mystery of art is that the art-work not only somehow and in a definite perspective points to personality and love, as the good deed in the field of ethics did, but that it brings the full abundance, the inexhaustible infinity of love and personality to the fore, absorbed totally and without residue in this its meaning. This distinguishes the art-work, indeed, from any other "valuable object." The "good work," as an instrumental value, disclosed the absolute goodness of a person only fragmentarily and in a limited perspective and, therefore, **pointed** merely to the person who, in his fullness, remained hidden and did not enter into the deed. The art-work, however, not merely points to a person outside of its orbit, it realizes the fullness of personality, it is real as this very realization, and we, confronted with it, are in the presence of this personality, share its life to the full and feel enriched by its abundance. We forget the "thing," the object, for the thing was not real; real was the creation, the structured process which lifted beyond the setting of the thing and revealed a unique and absolute life.

We call a work which only points to personality and

discloses this personality in a certain perspective a "good work." But we call a work which fully and in its abundance discloses goodness, the infinite reality of personality, a "beautiful work." Beauty is the structure which lives the ineffable and inexhaustible life of love and communion. No "good work" can give us the experience of being in the presence of and in a living communion with personality. But the beautiful art-work can. Beauty is the manifestation of goodness, but in a thing, and not only a partial manifestation as in the good work,[4] but the total manifestation of its abundance, and therefore alive. We muddle our terms if we speak of a "beautiful action," for the action is limited; or if we speak of a "beautiful soul," for the soul is no thing. Only things are beautiful, only works, and they are so when they disclose a whole person. We may call a human body beautiful, when we regard it as if it were a created work, and we can do this when the body has been marked by the experiences of the soul and radiates in face, movement and gestures the full life of the person—which the body rarely does. We may even call Nature as an inspiring object, f.i. a landscape, "beautiful," when we have abandoned all merely useful considerations with regard to it and see in it a creation in which we share because it discloses the unity of structure and process, is alive and reminds us of love as the core of all life. The beauty of Nature, therefore, has been discovered in its full intensity only after man had fathomed the World as the work of a loving Creator.

Beauty cannot be analyzed or defined, just as love, personality and the Good in ethics cannot be defined. The artwork in its abundance and inexhaustible richness of life is ineffable. There is an absolute truth in every great work of art, discovered by the artist as the structure of reality, manifested in his work. But this defies a conceptual statement; its only possible statement is the work itself, and its truth is known in the act of sharing. Beauty, like goodness, though indefinable, is experienced and known in the way love is known.

The love which is here concerned with a thing, a work, may remind us of the "care" in the ethical realm which was also concerned with a material object, a body; and in both cases the concern transcends the object and reaches beyond it toward a life, a person. The artist and his public "care for" the work of art, and their care lifts them in love beyond the work to a communion of response for which the work is a bridge. And just as in the ethical realm the bodily sphere was sanctified as the bridge to a spiritual union, so also here, in an even more conspicuous way, the material structure, the thing, the work, is made holy as an indispensable factor in the loving communion of beauty. The emphasis on an inward vision alone, not materialized in a structured object, would not do justice to the unique phenomenon of beauty and would deprive the loving communion of the mediating bridge which consolidates the union and grounds it in care and in the object of care. Through care as a medium of a material nature the ethical man found his bodily place; through care for the work of art again a material medium, a setting is given in which the spiritual aspirations of personalties meet. There is a truly ethical element in this care for the work of art, and thus this care is not merely concerned with an accomplished object to be preserved and protected, but with its unfolding from stage to stage, from tone to tone, entering into the process of its creation, meeting in this process, lovingly caring for every element as an embodiment of love. Every tone, every color, line or word is tenderly cared for and receives its place in the structure, confirmed and strengthened by the presence of every other element. Honesty and sincerity, so conspicuous in the field of human communion, are here present too. A work of art will touch and move because of this honesty and sincerity of care, taken for every element in its structure and—through this structure—for the persons who meet in the work, themselves confirmed and strengthened and given their place in the communion. Any superficial faking which provides a cheap enjoyment will be rejected and will frustrate rather than intensify the lives of those who are exposed to it. Such a frustration will arrest the artist and his public in the material sphere and so also here, like in ethics, shame will be felt because of this perversion.[5] We are indeed ashamed when we are exposed to an exhibitionist novel or to sweetish music, knowing that what should have been a bridge for reaching out to others has become an obstacle which makes sharing impossible. And "shyness," as a milder form of frustration, will put a barrier between artist and public when, in spite of a sincere effort, the meeting in the work did not "come off," because an awkward handling of the material, a weakness of care, erected a wall between artist and public. Just as in the ethical realm the body was cared for, but the person was loved, so also here the sensuously structured object is the immediate and indispensable object of care and perception, but leads beyond perception to a spiritual and creative communion. Enjoyment may be felt on the level of the sensuous object, colors, lines, sounds, texture and words, but the essential enjoyment is not with regard to these elements, but with regard to a new level of value. Who gets arrested in mere sensuous enjoyment, has not penetrated into the core of artistic beauty.

So, on the one hand, the sensuous object may become a danger, by arresting us in its superficial charm, just as man may get "infatuated" by the bodily appearance of a fellow-person, but, on the other hand: here is an object in space and time which becomes a scaffold for man's reaching above his enclosure into a spiritual communion. Certainly, for those who have the strength and vitality to enter immediately into the life of another person, art is not indispensable. But there are legions of people, who are fenced in and hopelessly isolated, and thus unable, to reach into other lives without the support of the art-object which, although of a sensuous nature, becomes the bridge and medium for a loving communion. Even in the religious sphere and for the communion of man and God art has been an invaluable help and intensification: music, painting, sculpture, drama and architecture opened man to a religious vision. But this is not all: Even for those who are able to form a union of love, unique and exclusive, their intercessional vocation, their representative mediation with all the people in need would not be achieved, if the artist did not close his profound experience in an object, open to everyone. The artist may himself not clearly be aware of his mission, but it is lastly this responsibility, not vanity and not the craving for recognition, which makes him express and render public what was his most intimate vision, and which is accepted by the public as a powerful aid to a loving communion. A silent prayer would be understood by God, it would not need any spoken words; a silent devotion would equally be felt by the beloved person: But the psalmist moulds his vision into words of depth and intensity, in order to open the road of redemption to the many, responsible as he is in his heart for all needy people around. Thus it is a temple built, in order that others may meet under its vault, a holy ground, to assemble and feel in union with each other. Not that the artist, who has received his inner vision, decides as an afterthought to make it public: It is one and the same act by which the artist experiences the living communion and by which he unfolds it in his work. His "having" and his "expressing" the vision is one indistinguishable process of devotion, a manifestation of the living communion itself. How could it be otherwise, considering that the call comes to him, just as it came to the religious man, from a future which is linked to a past, pregnant with this future, a tradition which is alive, because it is ready to be transformed. Thus the artist is deeply indebted to the living past of tradition, which inspired him and upon which he heavily drew, paying his debt to the past by giving to the future. The artist is, as the exponent of his culture, an instrument only for making explicit and for rendering public the accumulated treasure of the past. The prophecy of the artist is receiving and giving in unity, and it is therefore in and through the proceeding of his work that the communion unfolds, a communion which intercessionally includes all who are in the reach of his call. This prophecy may at times emphasize more the loving care for tradition, at times the dynamic sacrifice of this very tradition for the sake of a new future. We will have to return to this problem as the problem of "style."

The prophecy of the artist, whatever it may be, is always an intercessional representation of mankind, never merely concerned with the artist himself. Just like "selflove" was a perversion in the realm of ethics, so is "selfexpression" or "selfenjoyment" a perversion in art, eliminating the communion of lives, indispensable for the artistic value. A one-sided emphasis on the harmony of subjective functions, on the interplay of the artist's mental faculties, deprives art of its seriousness and responsibility and results in the disastrous "play-theory" of art. Play is self-enjoyment: child and man enjoy their own faculties by play. But it is not our own self which we enjoy in the great works of art, we enjoy our responsible communion with others in intercession and selfnegation. Hereby the neutral work, the detached object, helps detaching ourselves from the narrow enclosure in the fences of the ego and allows to transcend into a wider life of the communion. It may seem a paradox that a material object frees us from our material embodiment and helps us to transcend it in the direction toward a spiritual union. But this paradox loses much of its opacity when we remember that the object of culture is not a "material object," for on this level the distinction between matter and form has vanished as a mere abstraction. The art-work as one of the highest manifestations of culture is matter and form in a unity which defies both, and which in this unity becomes the object of unique care.[6]

It is for this reason that in every work of art "matter" is as important as "form," the "embodiment" being an indispensable factor, **not** to be minimized. The structured "material" object defies in its unity of form and matter any analysis. But as intelligent man has always to analyze, the art-critic has tried to find general standards of evaluation by tearing the art-object apart, in order to find in the dismembered work a clue for the effectiveness of the work. Since time immemorial such standards have been proclaimed and the dynamic uniqueness of the work turned into a pattern of typical abstraction, under headings like symmetry, proportion, repetition, balance etc. That there is a lawfulness, even a truth, in the work of art is undeniable, but it is a concrete and individual law, which has found its best expression in what we call "Style." The Style is a mysterious entity, never satisfactorily elucidated in the history of art. It points to the interwovenness of material texture and formative power and is a witness for the inseparable unity of matter and form, of necessity and freedom.

In the history of art the Style has at times become identified with "form" opposed to the material. But then it was soon discovered that an abstract form is not "Style" at all. So the analyzing mind turned to the material and tried to find the mystery of Style in the diversity of material. But this worked neither. The scholar had to resign in the statement that it is neither only form nor only material which constitutes Style, but that their integration, their inseparable and indistinguishable unity makes what we experience as style. In primitive times this unity is felt and naively carried out: therefore such primitive works have a powerful style. But when man becomes more sophisticated he begins to separate form from matter and he may study predominantly different possibilities of form. But as long as he is unable to embed these forms in their adequate material, which, in a way, calls for this kind of form, inspires this kind of form, he has no style. Only the mature artist after trial and error and by the labor of his experiences achieves again what the naive artist had done without failure: the integration of form and matter. A Michelangelo was inspired just as much by the block and the variety of human gestures as he was by any formative principle of "Contraposto," and so was Rembrandt just as deeply fascinated by the problems of color and of human suffering as he was by the balance of cold and warm colors and the display of volume. The mature and ingenious artist loses himself in the material as a source of inspiration. An abstracted form would be a mere "formula." Even that compromise between abstraction and imagination which we found on the level of daily life and which resulted in an average law of probability, is not Style, but provides merely the "Type." The consciousness of daily life functions in a typical manner. But neither the Style of the individual artist nor the "Style of the Age" is typical. The familiar typification of things and events is, when seen from the point of view which Style provides, a mere appearance, an "analogy" only to reality, as we have found it above,[7] while true reality is brought to light by "stylization," a reality, not merely "suggested" by appearances and images,[8] but grasped with unfailing immediacy by the style of the artist.

Conceptual abstraction and the stereotype appearance of life are however reductions, familiar in their humdrum-pattern of every-day, but deprived of the unique intensity and individuality which the style of the artist discloses. The artwork, therefore, never "imitates" this reduced kind of objectivity. Not the artist, but the scientist works in this reduced and analogical sphere and by reduction arrives at his generalizations and laws; the "practical" man equally reduces reality to that which is "useful"; the child reduces to the simple elements which it can grasp. In every reduction is an element of omission, of accidental and arbitrary simplification, and it is this arbitrariness which may provide a certain attraction, even a sensation and agreeable shock, when exaggerated, as a breach in the monotonous existence of every-day familiarity. The poster uses this exaggeration of reduction, and although the method is not totally different from the every-day-reduction, its exaggeration makes a great effect on the masses. Not reduction, but, on the contrary, intensification is the core of art. But reduction and simplification satisfy the crowd which may hail such a reduction to a formula also as a protection against the complexity of life and the insecurity which weak men feel in the face of it. Fear asks for simplification, as a haven against the unbearable onrush of life's dynamism. It cannot be denied that there are boundary-realms, where in times of transition and demonic fear the struggle of man with his destiny has whipped up passions and has given rise to an impressive but problematic style. Our own time, on the verge of disaster, has cherished this demonic expression and has fought its fears with means similar to magic and magical formulas, reductive and abstract. Dogmatism and fanaticism have appeared in the wake of this art and have gloried in school-battles, persecuting the opponent as a heretic, in a quasi-religious obsession, and proclaiming their truth as battle cries and universal pronunciamentos. It is by formulas of this kind that aggression and competition proceed and sharpen the antagonism of the fighters. Styles, on the other hand, never give rise to hostility, but strengthen each other in giving and taking, just as personalities, the more intensive and unique they are, become means of mutual unfolding. The way of the genius is characterized by his humble devotion to the styles of former times which lead him on his path toward maturity.

To every style belongs its subject matter; which has to be present, in order that its familiarity be overcome by stylization. Impressionism preferred as its subject matter the infinite variety of nature, expressed in landscape; other styles have indulged in other matters, as "Expressionism" has been attracted by the problems of the human soul. But with this emphasis on a subject matter, detachable from its form, the reign of "Style" is by no means yet exhausted: What we distinguish as "lyrical" or "epic" or "dramatic,' and in the latter group as "tragic" or "humorous," is a difference in style, and in none of these stylistic formations can the subject matter be neglected. The "lyrical" will treat the universal experiences of mankind, death, love, loneliness, but in spite of the subjective nature of these experiences they will pour out from an anonymous source, from a soul which reaches out beyond its isolation and represents the eternal aspirations of man. The "epical style" will organize an objective material of actions, works, events, reflectively drawn before the judgment of a present narrator, and thus it will trace a horizon, under the vault of which people will live, act and die. The "dramatic style," at last, will unfold a specific "plot," a dynamic development toward the future, toward the climax of fulfillment, and this climax will be "tragic," if the hero's action carries him to doom and sacrifice, which however reveal his destiny and invest him with sublime dignity. While there is a quiet unfolding of the present in the lyrical mood as well as in the epic reflection, the dramatic style unfolds in a direction toward the future, to a call. Just as in the religious sphere there was besides a tender preservation of the present a destructive and responsible call to the future,[9] so also here the difference in style makes for the joy of "beauty proper," on the one hand, and for a sublime, but destructive tragedy, on the other. Not always is the joy of beauty clearly set off against the tragic and sublime element in a work of art: They are interwoven in the greatest and most comprehensive works, in Mozart's tender but deeply moving melodies, in Bach's powerful glorification of a World the foundations of which are trembling under God's call, and in all those master works where life is seen with its death and its resurrection. The Sublime has always had its place besides the quiet beauty, and it has been since time immemorial one of the most intricate problems of art that it can be fully understood only in its twofold and contradictory character.

At last it is the "Comedy" with its humour and lightness, which must be recognized as a stylistic form of drama. Comedy unfolds a life in its tension and complexity and takes into account the human deficiencies besides the accomplishments, the failures linked to the virtues.[10] Thus comedy inflicts wounds and heals them, like tragedy did. But, indeed, the ways by which both reach beyond failure are very different. In tragedy it is the call, the vocation which asks the hero to accept failure, death, suffering and sacrifice for the sake of a resurrection on a higher plane. His faith points to a future which does not belong to the

World of suffering, but to a World beyond toward which he is courageously headed. Comedy, on the other hand, never leaves the World of facts, failure and accidental aberrations, but it lives a faith, a loving assurance that there will be a healing power in this very World of meaningless accidents, of unforeseeable coincidences, and of misfortune. It is this World in its nonsensical complexity which Comedy asks us to love and to believe in. Certainly there is something missing in the humorous evaluation of life: destiny, the call and deepest meaning of man are not present, and therefore we are inclined to regard Comedy as a deficient and somehow reduced, artificial presentation of the full abundance of life. But this is not quite fair. Surely the danger of artificiality is present, and Comedy may degenerate into a routine of tricks, into stereotype characters as "funny;" but if this happens, we are in the realm of farce, and not art. The humorous work as such is not stereotype; its characters are not really fixed and abstract, although they miss the highest nobility of personality, the readiness for sacrifice. A Don Quixote, a Mr. Micawber are not types, they are unique individuals, for art has use only for the unique; but as those characters remain somehow in the close structure of their environment, they may rather express the cultural setting to which they belong, than represent an absolute World of their own. Fairy tales too will express the humorous and humble love for human deficiencies, coupled with a faith not so much in the power of personality as in the healing power of this crazy World itself and its inherent forces.[11] Fairy tales will use, therefore, the help of ghosts, fairies, gnomes, as exponents of the mysterious friendly elements in a Nature which only seems to be hostile, and this seeming hostility will again be personified by natural forces, demons, giants, monsters, entering the story merely in order to be defeated. And so the human fellow will undergo with a naive faith all the inevitable failures and hardships, knowing that in the long run everything will be all right. It is, to put it into one single word, the life of "adventure" which the humorous Comedy and the Fairy Tale glorify. Man goes into the World in order to meet adventure, in order to "learn to fear" as a famous Fairy Tale announces, but knowing that no serious disaster awaits him, and that his fear will be an agreeable seasoning which will make life still more worthwhile. What ranges Comedy among the expressions of great Art, is the faith which it lives and conveys, a faith which is not altogether far from an awareness of God's mercy. It is not "superiority" which gives joy to the spectator of the human Comedy, as has been claimed at times; it is rather the humble faith in the healing power of life which the spectator feels even in moments when the comic hero himself seems at the end of his resources; and thus the spectator will be eager to expose himself to the same misadventure, because, far from feeling superior, he wants to share a delightful adventure which surely will have a happy end.

Tragedy and Comedy play on the same register of human frailty and may be regarded as two extreme swings of the pendulum. The tragic will give to the humorous aspect of life a veil of sadness, of sweet resignation, and the humorous confidence in the healing power of the World will soften the despair of tragic destruction and will make us smile through tears. Whoever empties life from its tragic and humorous elements impoverishes our vision, and this will indeed happen, when art discards subject-matter entirely. Whoever glories in "Art for Art's sake" cuts art off from its roots, from life with its tragedies and its humor. This perversion is only partly remedied, when art is explained as a "symbolic endeavor." Here life is allowed to enter, but merely as a field to which the symbol points. We had to reject symbolic explanation as inapt to do justice even to "Existence," [12] much more so here, where the highest level of reality is at stake. A symbol belongs to the abstract, conceptual order of truth, it "stands for" truth, anticipates and intends it. In doing this it may substitute for reality and thus confirm by its substitution the fact that reality itself is missing. In this way the symbol shuts out reality just as much as it points toward it, and it will lead finally to the resignation that life is out of reach; and so it will become a medicine for the spiritually sick. But in fact: the art work does not substitute, does not replace and eliminate life, it rather eliminates itself for the sake of life, and in sacrificing its own thinglike appearance it unfolds the higher reality of a spiritual life. The religious hymn, far from only substituting for a devotional reality, actually lifts man into this devotion; the novel makes the reader enter into the very life which the story discloses; the drama opens the barren heart to a unity with others and allows the spectator to mature in the intensity of his experience. If art were only a symbol, pointing merely to a meaning beyond itself, then the church would not have needed it; its own symbols, its rituals would have served to full satisfaction. But, indeed, the ritual was deficient, the "sacrament" had to take its place, the embodiment, the incarnation of the holy, the sacrificial sublimation, which as stylization is essential also to the work of art, a sacramental embodiment, not a symbol.[13] It was because of this sacramental nature of art that Western civilization, after the secularization of religion in modern times and after the surrender to technology, could preserve its spiritual heritage: Religion lived on in great music dramas, in powerful architecture, in dynamic paintings, in poetry and novel. Technology was not strong enough to absorb these immense spiritual forces which in their turn took technical inventions into their service. If ever religion has a rebirth, it owes the possibility of its renewal to the great Western art which held the spiritual fort in times of a tremendous materialistic aggression.

It will now be our task to enter more explicitly into the nature of this "sacramental" offering which art presents. If we remember that all sacrifice is a destruction on the lower level and a preservation of the destroyed on a higher one, then we understand that the elements which are destroyed but sublimated and thus preserved are "matter" and "form," which, integrated with each other, undergo a new unity. What is destroyed here is the abstract and familiar object, its conceptual pattern of words, of symbols, the mere content of consciousness. In poetry the pattern of words with their familiar meaning gives way to a new understanding, rising out of the mutual destruction of the abstract and fixed concepts, out of the discrepancy of their interrelation, out of disharmony and tension. We call this tension and creation of a new meaning "metaphorical" because it "carries beyond" the original and narrow word-meanings. The typical concepts undergo a "communion" with each other, very different from a mere "relation," a communion which reveals the tension of life as a concrete and unique truth, radiating uniqueness even into the single concepts transcended in the metaphor. It may seem that the single concepts thus lose some of their clarity and universality in the communion, but they gain a heightened universality, problematic with regard to the familiar words, but open to a new insight, simple in spite of the complexity of the tension and shared in this simplicity. Here destruction is indeed at work in creation, but what is destroyed is only the abstract and narrow fixity of qualities and concepts, and what is won is the substantial ground and fundamental meaning, which were hidden by the surface pattern of accidents and symbols. Substance and meaning are present and disclosed in the metaphorical interaction and mutual destruction. They are revealed in a dynamic tension, complex in its elements, but simple in our experience which builds on words, but transcends words. This experience is a truth, a knowledge, but not as a content over against a consciousness, but **one** with the consciousness, matter **one** with form and thus alive. The reader or spectator **lives** this metaphorical ground; he is not simply conscious of it; he is involved in it, he is intensified by it in his being, for he has entered into the substantial and meaningful ground of his own existence.[14]

The phenomenon which we have tried to analyze as the "metaphor of speech" has, however, a much wider field of application. In fact, this phenomenon is the clue to all art and creation. In every work of art familiar and abstract fixations are welded into a living communion, in which their isolated meaning is destroyed in order to give birth to a higher meaning and reality. In this wider application the metaphorical tension may be called by another general term: "Rhythm." Rhythm is a communion of separate entities which lose in the communion their isolated nature and acquire a new reality. What we have investigated with regard to words, holds true with tones, colors and lines; everywhere rhythm makes the core of creation, and everywhere it is a transformation and sublimation of isolated natural and abstract entities into a communion of a unique and concrete life. In their isolation these entities follow in the dimensional pattern of time and space; but rhythm lifts out of this pattern, welds space and time together and transcends and fulfills them in the superdimensional sphere of pure intensity, which, in the integration of spatial and temporal rhythm, may be called a "Melody."

Melody in its widest meaning as a melody of tones, words, colors and lines, is an indistinguishable unity of content and form. In the interaction of its entities no distinction can be made between a material on the one hand, and a formative power on the other: it is as if the material itself gave rise to its form, or as if the formative rhythmic power created its own material, as God created His matter. A distinction between form and matter is valid on the conceptual and sensuous level; but the rhythm of melody has transcended senses and concepts. Here not even a distinction can be made between substance and its accidents. There is no substantial "thing" to be abstracted in the course of the rhythm as if it were the carrier of an accidental sequence of changes. It is the rhythm itself which is substance as well as an "accidental" sequence of changes, its tension as such is the substantial power, present in the multiple, changing entities, not distinguishable from the rhythm itself. The oneness of matter and form, of process and structure, of subject and object, of the accidental and the substantial, is the essential character of rhythm and melody and constitutes its unique simplicity. Here is no flux of images—although the word "rhythm" means literally flux—and here is no blurring of these images into a content, unified by consciousness. The vitalistic imagination should not be confused with the creative imagination of rhythm. Instead of a neutral consciousness, welding the fleeting phases together by memory and expectation, every single rhythmic entity is here a center of unity, forming as well as being formed by every other entity, each one a creator and a creature. And although every element is set off sharply from every other, not blurred as in the fleeting sphere of life, it nevertheless reaches out into other and always other elements, in a tightness and intensity of communion, quite unlike the loose flow and sequence of images. Here is not a unity imposed upon a multiplicity of forms, it is rather so that the manifold creates its own unity as well as splits itself up in abundance. Not unity is in the foreground of attention, while the many enter only as a material for structuring, as this is the perspective which the scientist adopts: the creative artist cherishes rather the abundance of modifications, spending himself, giving himself in ever new ways. Expansion, not reduction, is his aim. We may point here as an example to the musical "variation": a "theme" will serve here as an underlying unity, but this theme becomes alive and fulfills itself in the abundance of its variations. The scientific mind will be happy to detect the identity of the theme in all the different modifications, as if this were what mattered. But the musician knows and the listener understands that it is the variety and not the unity of the theme which is the meaning of his creative attempt. The tension which the melody presents is not so much a tendency toward unity as a tendency to spread out and to split this unity into an abundant manifold. But to be precise: it is neither the one nor the many, for no quantitative consideration is here adequate. It is the "Simple" which lifts up and delights; for the Simple is an expression of "Force," a concentration, the more intensive as it gives birth to an evergrowing abundance of manifestations. Only "Force" is simple, as a center of expansion, of outreach, and creativity. And here we have arrived again at the idea of Force, which rose as an ideal before the mind, when abstraction tried to heal the split between law and instances, purpose and means, and which moved into the center of our search and revealed itself as the core of reality, when personality and communion conquered the field.[15] Personality, indeed, is a unity of force, contained in itself, but in spite of this self-containedness reaching out to other personalities in the tension of a loving communion. This self-containedness and this reaching out characterizes also rhythm and melody, where each tone is absolute as a **force**, uniquely centered in itself, but at the same time it manifests its absoluteness in its outreach to other tones with which it constitutes a dynamic communion. Melody may be understood as an encounter of forces which mutually intensify each other, and it is this encounter of forces into which we enter enlivened, strengthened as personalities when drawn into this dynamic communion. Melody is not experienced in the way of knowledge, enjoyment or appreciation; it is **lived.** Our own life comes to a more vivid awareness of its power and outreach when involved in rhythmical dynamism. We live, when partaking in the rhythm of melody, the uniqueness and richness of a heightened existence, being embedded in a World which carries us, and at the same time embedding this World in the vivid awareness of our creativity. It is this absolute World of interacting forces, this communion of mutually intensified living centers of power which makes it possible that men find themselves in unity with each other when merged into and inspired by the rhythm of a universally valid melody.

Every tone of a melody, as a unique center of power and outreach, is a forward thrust toward a future, irresistibly luring on; but every tone also holds on to itself and, although leading to the future, refuses to become a past. In this unique encounter of forces future and past are welded into a present in which every element as "past" receives its character from an element of the "future," and every element which is still to come is foreshadowed by those which have passed. In this balance the melody "stands" as a dynamic present, and can, because of this, be shared only in the totality of its tones, in the indivisible presence of its structure and process. Melody has its own specific indivisibility which, unlike the indivisibility of the space-time-given, does not reject division, but builds its indivisible tension on the manifoldness of its structure, one with its manifoldness in spite of its indivisible unity. There is not a sequence of homogeneous here-nows as extended, and there is not a "momentum" as a center of intensity, from which powers radiate backward and forward, fading in as much as they lose themselves in past and future. There is no "anticipation," no expectation of probabilities, for the process, though apparently in sequence, "stands" in the unbreakable present of its dynamic structure, just as the communion of personalities stands in the ever present structure of its value. And as there is no anticipation which would counteract the creatively new, "suspense" is excluded too, and so is "surprise" as the sudden resolution of suspense. Neither suspense nor surprise have a place in the melody, they belong rather to the material, sublimated in the rhythm of the melodious present.[16] The inspired vision which allowed Mozart to face the whole composition at once in one dynamic unity transcends as well the violent ruptures between past and future as also the compromising blending of both on the level of life and "mood." On the contrary, such a "standing" of the melody in its dynamic present may recall the experience of religious men: the Eternal. There is a "fulfillment of time" in the unity and present of melody, transcending all dimensions, as this was felt and dreamt of in eschatological visions. Melody, fulfilling time, absorbs indeed the whole dimensional sphere, whenever it is heard. It is in process and yet stable; unfolding and yet at rest, and, although building on elements measurable by beat and intervals, it is itself beyond measurement; it is infinite and thus lifts to a height where man experiences the eternal forces which hold him in an ever-renewed communion of love.

Only when this unity is achieved, the work "stands" actually in its fulfilled present, in its "eternity," a presence which is at rest. But it is not only at rest, it keeps also on evolving in an unending motion. It is this motion which we have now to consider as an essential feature beside the firm structure of the work. This motion, seemingly temporal, guides our eye in a sweep, when we, faced with a "spatial" architectural interior or with a picture, unfolds and builds up the structure. The way we take in the coexisting elements is not left to our arbitrary choice as if this process were an activity foreign to the art-work as such. When we trace an empirical object, a tree or a house, we are indeed left to our arbitrary choice: we are allowed to start wherever we like, at the left or right, at the bottom or the top. But this is not so with a work of art. Who has ever entered the nave of a Gothic cathedral knows that here no rambling movement is allowed to our eyes, no strolling through space, in order to make us conscious of its beauty. We will be drawn irresistibly into a current of forces, driven along the lines of nave and vault, in a tempo dictated by the rhythm of these lines. And the same holds true with regard to any masterwork in the field of painting, where again the eye is led in a definite path, in order to trace the surface and depth of the work. But even this is not all: when the spatial structure has been rounded off in a successive rhythm, the dynamic motion does not stop, for it was not meant as a merely psychic device of perception only. The motion goes on indefinitely in the mind of the spectator, sinking into the depth of his being and intensifying the rhythm of his life. Melody is, whatever art it represents, a structure as well as a process, stable as a structure, dynamic as a process, and it is this process which renews itself without end. The work of art is "alive" and we are involved in the process of this life; it is real only as long as it lives in the process and rhythm of our experience. "Creation" is structure and process at once, and so the spectator's activity plays a part in this creation, which is real not as a "music-piece" or a colored canvas, but as a living performance and experience of personality.

Abstraction and analysis, are foreign to the artwork and its "melody," [17] as an integration of temporal and spatial rhythm. Only by isolating the temporal rhythm and the spatial rhythm can abstract rules be tentatively detected for each of them: the laws concerning the temporal sequence of tones, of long and short, of accentuation, of tone-lines and of the structure of movements; furthermore the spatial rules of harmony, of the distance between high and low tones, and the possibility of their effect. But if the artist indulges in one of these rhythms, the temporal or the spatial, at the expense of the other, then the work will have only a limited value; it will appear in need of supplementation, it will at best be an "accompaniment" and can be used as such, it will have an "ornamental" function.[18] No masterwork will be like this, and when we, in our analytic inclination seem to acknowledge arts which express only one of the part-rhythms, when we speak of "spatial arts," meaning architecture, sculpture and painting, and of "temporal arts" like music, dance and drama, we use a loose language. For none of these arts fructifies only the part-rhythm of its label. There are no dimensions in the fullness of melody. Painting expresses not only the spatial rhythm of color, of dark and low or of bright and high colors, but it welds this spatial rhythm to the temporal rhythm of lines, drawn in a way which makes our eyes follow quickly or slowly according to the swift smoothness or groping raggedness of the contour. And similarly in music, as a temporal art, the emphasis on temporal rhythm, on accentuation, on tone-sequence and "contour" will have to be supplemented by a rich harmony of tone-distances. The development of western music has even been guided and hurried forward by nothing so much as by the polyphonic togetherness of toneliness, by harmony and counterpoint, by spatial breadth and depth of melody. It will not be too audacious to make the following statement: in spatial arts it was the temporal element, in temporal arts the spatial element which had to be emphasized to the utmost in order to become responsible for the historical advance.[19] Just as in music the harmonic voice-leading, the spatial polyphony, was responsible for the extraordinary development, so in poetry and drama, as temporal arts, the road to maturity did not lead over an increasing complexity of the plot, of the temporal chain of events, but rather over a growing richness of breadth and width which the hero's character either by its own expansion or by its expansion into other characters provided, as a quasi-spatial medium for the carrying out of the plot. In sculpture and architecture as "spatial arts," on the other hand, the temporal factor of contour-rhythm in its smooth swiftness or groping raggedness became decisive and determined the style and its unfolding. Similarly in painting it was the temporal conduct of lines, of the drawing, which seemed so important in the development of this art that art historians regarded those cultural periods as artistically prominent and ranked them above the others, in which draughtsmanship had been leading, like in the Florentine and Roman Renaissance. This is the more astonishing as color, light and shadow are the essence of painting and the profoundest expression of personality, maturing in the experience and wisdom of age, so that at the height of their life men like Titian and Rembrandt found the full subtlety and richness of their color-vision, while draughtsmanship may find a master also among the young.

Only when the part-rhythms of space and of time are balanced with each other and integrate into each other in an inseparable unity of melody, the greatness of art will be revealed.[20] This greatness will ask for an unparalleled depth of emotional experience, very unlike the feelings and moods we found on the vitalistic level, where they preserved each other in a tension of opposites, anxiety, astonishment, despair on the one hand, and hope, joy and triumph on the other. These feelings will accompany imaginative man in his actions, hurt or satisfy, stir up and disturb the complacent tranquility of his humdrum life. But the arousing of such feelings is not the task of art. As long as man remains on this level, his reaction to art will be of a subjective kind, he will "feel" differently according to temperament and past experience. But when melody has taken hold of him, he will be lifted out of his subjective feelings and will be carried into the depth of an emotion, objective and universal. It was Kant who discovered late in life the reality of such objective and universal emotions in the field of art. This emotion may be termed "Faith" or—as stated before— "love," and it will unite man with man, when carried by the power of melody, unmistakenly and unerringly.

In this depth of faith and love man takes care of man: no "distance" or "disinterestedness" does justice to the attitude of the artist. It is rather the scientist, the scholar who remains in distance to the world, disinterested in the manifold aspects of things and concerned only with the reduced pattern of his lawful generalizations. The artist cannot withdraw from the concrete and infinitely varied experiences of life, although he will lift himself above the petty worries of everyday existence. But he will do this only, in order to be more deeply involved and concerned about the agonies, the hopes and sufferings, the tragedies of his fellowmen. In responsibility he will share intensely the experiences of man, the world will enter his heart; and the dramas which are open to him because of the width and depth of his personality will become a part of his very own life. Not unlike the ethical man he has to live up to an infinity of demands; he is not allowed to spare himself and to seek protection behind the narrow walls of his personal existence. Not aloofness, but sensitivity is the mark of the inspired person, and this sensitivity is an open door to the abundance of the World, purified, however, and concentrated in an ingenious vision. There may be an inclination on the part of the artist to go on and on in shaping ever-new versions of his experience, forming ever-new attachments, new commitments which he is unable to discard, and so he will spend himself freely and unsparingly, forgetting his comfort, his needs, in a devotion which burns away every shred of self-indulgence and relies on the force of inspiration, flowing indefinitely and taking shape in ever-new works.[21] When, instead of this inspiration, a meager scheme of rules serves as a starting ground, then the artist will indeed be deprived of the generosity of his abundant spending and will meanly fill his narrow frame, anxious to achieve an illusionary "perfection."

But the generosity of the "genius"—for this is what we call a genius—should not be confused with wastefulness and lack of responsibility. Here the "Bohemian" is the caricature of true genius. The true genius has an awareness of responsibility greater than the average man: he is faced with the impossible, with the task of catching and holding Infinity in a finite structure. As the great scholar is faced by the "Unknowable" as his responsibility, driving him on his search, so the artist is faced by the "Impossible" which lays a strain upon him, unbearable, if his inspiration were not the power to carry him courageously forward toward a fulfillment of that which seemed impossible. Desire, passionate desire, colors the activity of the artist; but what distinguishes his desire from the desire of the scholar is that grace is given him, not unlike the religious man. He will gratefully and humbly acknowledge that the accomplishment of his work surpassed his own limited possibilities, and that "inspiration" as a grace came to him from a beyond. What he had to do was to give himself to the task, in faith giving, spending, alienating his treasures for the work which is the work, not of "self-realization," but of welding his life and the life of others into a communion of love. The abundance and generosity of art is the attempt to embrace the infinity of personalities in a communion in which everybody can share. Communication is the core of art; its vision and inspiration is a vision of communicating, of expressing and exteriorizing, in order that all can meet on this ground. The working out of the vision is not simply a technical matter, watering down the concentrated visional power; it is the proceeding of the vision itself which is here the tendency to communicate by external means and to show "care" in the conscientious and tender way by which it handles its material.

This devotion and humble service is, however, what distinguishes the artist from the spectator or listener, as close as their union in the work may be. The artist will be driven by his responsibility and care for every single element in the work, he will be firmly rooted in his human concern, in his service, in need, in care, in the ups and downs of life, and, although his vision will again and again lift him above conflict and sacrifice, he will be near to the ethical man and his sacramental existence. He will not, it is true, like the doer, fall back behind his intention and will not be forced to cope with ever-new situations by ever-new decisions of his will—his work will be **one** with the infinite intention itself, with the life of the communion of which it is the full expression, and so he will be carried by his vision beyond tragedy and suffering. But as much as this may be so, the artist will need his most intensive effort in order to keep unwaveringly on the height of his creativity. His public, however, not faced with any struggle, not chained to any service in anxiety and hope, will easily be lifted into the full abundance of the inspired work; but it will slip down again all too quickly to normal stature. In this way the listener may be dangerously carried so far beyond the human situation, that he may, in his joy of the Divine harmony, not only forget his own sorrows, but also the sorrows and agonies of his neighbor. As long as his elevation lasts, he may be aloof to suffering, and it is this indifference which has rightly been blamed on the "aesthete." An aesthetic pantheism has even entered the religious realm, has at times made creator and creature melt into one inseparable unity and has destroyed prophetic transcendence, call, future and responsibility. Whether the religious experience of the East really went to rest in such a mystical all-unity, may be doubted; but it is beyond question, that the West restored the distance beween God and man, the communion, the prophetic action and man's responsibility for a messianic future. Western Art, fructifying this religious vision, cherished the tragic element in its most profound expressions of human life, avoiding the danger of aloofness and of a contentment not fitted for man.

On this religious ground of a loving communion the generosity of the genius and the devotion of his public meet. The listener or spectator will in this meeting be lifted beyond his petty everyday concerns, and will be open to the needs of his fellowmen and to activities, not channeled by utilitarian considerations. He should and will be eager to serve, for service, not enjoyment of indifference and aloofness, is the road along which art leads. It was Shakespeare who recognized the profoundly ethical nature of art and condemned the stranger to the muses as a brute and as a victim to criminal and cruel instincts. The sensitivity which Aristotle regarded as the mark of genius and which finds expression in compassion and love, is the atmosphere in which art is born, the medium by which men open their hearts to men and by which men become more lovable to men.

Here, at the end of our journey, a last and final truth may be stated: wherever there is a unity, it will overflow, radiate, reach out and break the dams which separate man from man. Not only is all rhythm lastly a fetter only in order to break forth into an abundance of ever-new expressions which enable an infinite number of personalities to widen their life infinitely; also the communion of love closes up in a unity in order to carry beyond its narrow boundaries the very love which its members feel for each other. So it happens that the loving communion of friend with friend, of husband with wife, of parents and children, point beyond their enclosure toward all the lives in their reach. The union between God and man, finally, opens up in the intercession of prayer which includes in its scope all those lives which are in need. There is no unity which does not overflow, opening toward the infinite possibilities of service and love.

CONCLUSION

Abstraction and Reality, things and life, laws and forces, everywhere the dualism of two Worlds breaks forth, raising problems, disturbing, but stimulating and tending to a unity in which the breach is healed. It is philosophy which discovers the breach, wonders in perplexity, and starts toward the solution. Cautiously and humbly philosophy reflects and clarifies the issue and points in the direction in which the solution may lie. It can only prepare the field, however, leaving to the individual the responsibility to make the ultimate steps. This was what Plato saw and described in his seventh letter.

The clarity, precision and exactitude which abstraction provides has become the ideal for man. Disappointments have grown out of this unattainable goal. Life has its own standard and, although it pays the price of having to abandon the precision of abstract formulas and laws, it is amply compensated by the absoluteness of its values and the certainty of a shared truth. It is "faith" in which the activities of life are grounded, faith as the fundamental experience in religion, ethics and art.

Knowledge is knowledge of things, relations and laws. Faith is faith in life, personality and love. Consciousness is their common denominator, consciousness of content, of objects on the one hand, consciousness of direction, of an unfolding and growth on the other. The Christian era marks the transition of emphasis from the one to the other. Paul declares in his passionate and powerfully suggestive way that love has taken the place of law; that law raises crime, but that love carries beyond deficiency, sin and even death. And from this time on, man has been lifted once and for all onto a new level of reality which sheds its light on abstraction, things and accomplishments and makes them shine in a new color. Abstraction is not cancelled, not eliminated and should not be regarded as an activity antagonistic to life. On the contrary, a true evaluation of life will disclose the service which abstraction, and only abstraction, is able to render life. Reason receives dignity through life, and life stability through reason. Order is meaningful only when allowed to serve the directed unfolding of life, which, without this service, perishes in anarchy. Order and organization, in themselves neutral and bare of value, become instrumental values when necessary conditions for the carrying out of life's tasks. Reason may miss its role, and organization may frustrate life; systems may smooth down the responsibility of the religious and ethical man, facilitate the making, instead of the creating, of works of art. Self-justification may creep in and substitute security for freedom, the "good conscience" for the disturbing but intensifying awareness of sin and guilt, and deprive man of grace and the incomparable height which it grants. This all may happen, but if it does, it is a perversion of reason, not the manifestation of its intrinsic structure. Rightly used, reason disciplines for freedom, sets the necessity for the breaking forth of free possibilities, prepares the field for a loving service.

Man will easily err and fail. He is a rational and he is also an imaginative and emotional being. Between these two powers he may become arrested and confused, and he may try to escape into pure reason, into pure abstraction, in order to evade the dangers of going astray. But this road of escape sacrifices too much. In eliminating imagination and emotion the road to life is cut off. But, on the other hand: life leads nowhere, when reason is shut out or debased. One may substitute mathematical order for reality, as Descartes may have intended; one may, turning in the opposite direction, regard the emotional powers as the only reality as Schopenhauer started to do, when he called his irrational and sinister pseudo-reality the "Will," although it was rather the disintegrating and self-destructive process of compulsion. But all these distorted and one-sided views are escapes from the fundamental but problematic interaction of life and reason.

Faith and knowledge belong together as soul and body do. The World of the body, the object-world, includes all finite beings, whether sensuously or intellectually apprehended. The emphasis on sense versus intellect is a psychological not a philosophical perspective, and has long enough in the history of thought usurped the place of the truly fundamental dualism: the finite versus the infinite.

The soul as infinite power is not set over against the finite body, nor is there any "relation" between soul and body, for relations are possible only between finite entities, belonging to the same sphere. The soul has to be understood as the force which manifests itself in and through the body. We "believe" in the force, and we "know" the manifestations. But these manifestations do not ever exhaustively "explain" the force behind them. Only in sharing the life of a person can we understand his soul. The reality of the soul, of personality, and its communion is the full reality, from which the body receives derivative and contingent existence, a servant to the soul, passing in this service through many stages of organizing knowledge and emotional expression.

Soul has not its locus in the body, nor outside of it. Its status prohibits any material and spatial determination. We may, however, regard the body as the soul's body, whereby our body as the closest environment may expand beyond the physiological boundary into a wider and ever wider structure of service, of things which "belong" to the soul and manifest the soul's power. But never can it happen that material things vanish and become fully absorbed in the power of the soul; the "nought" of creation will preserve a multitude of things apart from the creative spirit. Mythology and idealism have in vain tried to dissolve the world of things in a Divine spirituality. But in this way the Creator himself was in danger of disappearing together with his world of things, together with his creation. But, on the other hand, we may be allowed to regard the world of things as having only a "diminished reality," when seen in the light of personality and its communion of love. Therefore certainty is not to be found in the sphere of this diminished reality, not in the sphere of things, known by appearance and imagination. Here abstraction can only provide a hypothetical knowledge in the simplified but fragmentary structure of its laws. True certainty belongs to the realm of the soul, of personality and its communion—that is, to faith. This certainty is not about things, it is a certainty of direction in a life of service. The things which show up in the course of such a directed life will again and again be undermined by doubt which, however, intensifies the faith, the certainty of the way and its direction, as a testing ordeal through which the soul has to pass. Ambition and vanity and all the other passions which follow in the wake of things known and things doubted, failure and success, despair and pride, will color our struggle; but an undefeated Will rises ultimately to the certainty of faith.

Certainty is not security. Certainty is spiritual, security

material. The confidence which certainty provides is no insurance with regard to the steps to be taken in the realm of things. In the service of personality things have to be risked, surpassed and if necessary destroyed, besides being built up and confirmed by the service. The direction alone prevails, the intention of service; the steps have to be taken for what they are worth, suggestions for the future, proposals which life will have to correct. There is risk and adventure, but these risks and adventures are meaningful when undergone in the service of love.

No asceticism, no total extinction of things does justice to reality. For the things of the world are sanctified in the "care" through which we reach beyond them, and through which we are helped in finding and holding the right direction. More than anything else, our loving care for the bodily needs of our neighbour is a strong protection, providing a place from which we can, as from a firm stronghold, expand beyond any temporal and spatial seclusion. The world is a sacrament, when it is sanctified by care for the lives in our reach. This sacramental nature of the world is made supremely evident in the works of great art, in rhythm and melody as an embodiment of love and care.

This care and the sacramental holiness of things point to that which these things mean in the sphere of communion and personality. It is a tragic failure and misunderstanding to try, by possessing things, bodies, art-works, to draw an independent value out of them. They are sacrificial objects; they exist in order to vanish in that which they disclose. Our attitude to them should be a tender leave-taking, even in the moment when we are most deeply concerned about them and struck by their beauty. They are given to us in order to be spent, and not to be hoarded.

There is no possession in the realm of faith. Knowledge possesses but faith "has" only in order to spend. Faith follows the Chinese proverb: "Only the things we give away do we keep forever." Its wealth is its power of spending. Love spends, gives away, even its power to condemn and to forgive. That which alone remains and in remaining grows is the communion of life as the ground and meaning of all that is real.

NOTES

Chapter I

1. This absolute fact which thought does not think, but from which thought withdraws and which manifests the limitation of thought, closed to thought although belonging to thought, has found a parallel treatment in Kant's "thing in itself," which is no thing, but a problematic entity in the presence of which thought is silenced.

2. This emergence of an unquestionable fact out of the negating process of thought is the ultimate meaning, hidden in the Cartesian: "Dubito ergo sum."

3. Aristophanes "Birds" (693ff), where the night gives birth to the world-egg. See also on the orphic mystery Aristotle, Metaphysics 1071 b 27.

4. As the "relation of opposites" it played an important role in the thought of Anaximander, Pythagoras, Heraclitus, Anaxagoras, and even still in the thought of Aristotle.

5. This assimilation of fact and process will happen whenever fact and process meet, as a tentative but deficient attempt to reconcile the mutually excluded elements: Not only Being and Not-being are in this way assimilated and appear both as different kinds of being, but also "thing" and "motion," and, similarly "essence" as a stable fact and "existence" as a dynamic entity. Everywhere the disturbing and

excluded element, the processual Non-being, motion and existence will turn out as an assimilated kind of Being, thing and essence, until a profounder unity between fact and process comes to the fore.

6 This "vanishing" of terms which have lost their status and have become somehow "irreal" is a last residue of the "negative element." The terms are here negated as factual and independent entities in order to serve the unity of the identifying structure.

7. Philebus, 27 b and 64 d, e; and Timaeus, 28a.

8. See chapter VIII.

9. The English and French languages express this unity of a static structure and a dynamic structuring by words ending with "ion," like communion, construction, or organization, relation, creation. The German language uses the ending "ung" for the same purpose, as in Verbindung, Beziehung, Ordnung, Schoepfung, etc. The identity of fact and process is so fundamental that language as the earliest receptacle of wisdom could not pass it by.

10. When identity is expressed by the doubling of one and the same fact: "A is identical with A," then we are faced with an empty manoeuvre which merely uses the shell of the relation of exclusion in separating the fact from itself, as if the fact were in opposition to itself, but then finds it easy to return to unity, because the exclusion had only been a technical device. When we call a thing, awkwardly, "identical with itself," we really transform the thing into an order-structure, in which its various aspects take their separate place for the sake of being identified in the structure. We may elucidate this by pointing as an illustration to the Platonic idea: This idea is raised as an absolute structure of order over all its various examples which as such are unreal and vanish in the only real idea, in which they are identified.

11. The syllogism which plays a great role in traditional logic is but another way of expounding the principle of identity. The middle term unifies the other terms under its identifying frame: "S under M is P." We should therefore not be vexed when the syllogism turns out to be circular, the conclusion being included and already present in the premise. S and P disappear in M, because they are contained in M anyhow, and their separation was only a means to recover their unity.

12. See Meyerson; "Identity and Reality," where the author emphasizes the fundamental ground of identity in science.

13. It seems doubtful whether analogy can be fruitfully used when finite concepts and their order are at stake. We mentioned above (footnote 10) the Platonic idea and interpreted it as an order-structure under which the exemplars are identified. The modern "class-concept" has preferred analogy to identity, and has regarded the class as that kind of loose and vague unity which connects analogical order-structures, every exemplar seen as an order-structure of its own. We will have to cope with the problem of the "Universal" which is broached in the Platonic idea and in the modern class and we will have to try our own solution to this important and difficult problem, discarding analogy as well as identity and introducing instead "symbolization." (p. 52).

14. The early Greek school of Megara excluded rightly "possibility" from the logical realm which it regarded as factual in its necessity, and it was Diodorous Kronus who laid this principle down. If possibility must be introduced in the logical realm, it can only concern the non-factual terms of the relation of identity, those terms which lack the necessity of the structure and vanish in it. Thus we may speak of these terms as if they were possibilities of indiffer-

ence, of a readiness to disappear and to give up their separate and quasi-distinct status; or we may call them possible in the sense of non-contradictory or compatible. But if we use possibility in this way, we should be aware that it is a pseudo-possibility without any distinct character of its own, describing merely the non-factual nature of the logical terms and employing a word which has its proper place in another realm. Such a use can be justified only by the wish to bring two different realms close together, by a systemizing device, as St. Thomas used indeed his "possibile logicum," which as indifferent to fact was raised to the role of a presupposition to all facts, to all "creatio," and showed up as the "nihil" in God's intellect preceding His "creatio."

Chapter II

1. The equal power of part and whole will become an essential facet of those wholes which as "causes" enter into everyday-events; here every part will as a "given" infinity express the power of the whole and allow us therefore to regard such a part as a total fulfillment to rest in. (p. 37)

2. See also p. 57.

3. It was the Pythagorean Philolaos who discovered the possibility, essentially residing in the number (Diels, Fragments 11). That Infinity also was detected in the number by the Pythagorean school, was mentioned above, and so was the factor of negation. As the negation plays a fundamental role in number as well as in the atom, the kinship between both was early recognized. Aristotle compares the thought of the "atomists" with that of the Pythagoreans. (De Coelo 303a8).

4. The infinite regress can not be doubted with regard to numbers, but it has haunted philosophers in the causal realm of things and events, where we will have to question

it. (p. 38). But as the infinite regress is essential to numbers, it may be inadequate to close every number in the isolation of a "class," as this is done by modern theories.

Chapter III

1. Because of its non-abstract character intuition has at times been turned over to sensation, and this was done by those who know no other channels of experience but abstraction and sensation. But the Given is not sensed, it is neither seen, nor touched nor smelled.

2. We have used here terms of a non-abstract character like "maintenance" and "rejection" instead of abstract terms like "affirmation" or "negation." But the Given is indeed not an abstract entity and thus abstraction can cope with it only by surrendering to perspectives which point beyond the merely abstract. Abstraction as derivative will always more or less depend on elements not totally explainable by abstract terms and so we were faced right at the start of our investigation with "will" and "sacrifice."

3. See footnote 1 of Ch. II.

Chapter IV

1. Difference has at times been defined as "partial negation" and so the statement was made that "determinatio est negatio." But if this were true, no real distinction would ever be possible, for such a distinction would presuppose a negation of everything else. But even if this could be achieved, which it can not, such a negative distinction would not tell anything positive about the thing itself. Negation has the important task to protect against error, and we will treat it in this context. Thus difference and finiteness—the latter often characterized also as negative—can

under certain circumstances have a negative coloring, but only as a warning against an impending transgression into error.

2. Meyerson (Identity and Reality) regards the law of identity as the main structure of scientific systematization, minimizing in this way the differentiation which the instances provide.

3. Positivists have minimized the truth-value of laws in regarding them as mere expedient tools of organization. On the other hand, they have exaggerated the importance of law-knowledge as the only meaningful knowledge, ridiculing as nonsensical statements which are not verifiable. But only law-knowledge as a tension between the universal and the particular needs verification in order to unite them with each other. Knowledge which does not divorce the universal and particular is in no need of verification and would regard such a verification as not only superfluous but even as meaningless.

4. This distance is not a negation, concepts and laws are not "non-being." We had to reject the attempt to explain by negation before, when difference and finitude were at stake.

5. Stoicism discovered the symbol and used it amply also in Ethics as its main concern. Man as a symbol of the Cosmic process was absolute and fulfilled in his particularity the world-process, a free necessity with regard to the events of his life which were predications of him as the underlying subject. But, on the other hand, man as a symbol was also a mere intention, subordinated to the Cosmos which as fate ruled over him and his environment.

6. That concepts "have" meaning, "have" being and are in so far anticipations of truth is at the bottom of the "Correspondence"—theory of truth. That concepts, however, also "intend" being and are also on an infinite road to truth,

is emphasized by the "Coherence-theory." Each one of these theories contains and emphasizes one aspect of truth.

7. Symbols are not "signs," although both, symbols and signs may be united. The words of our languages are conceptual symbols with meaning, and insofar meet in this meaning, but as signs they are different, conventional and arbitrary. Whoever learns a foreign language has to memorize the signs and the syntax of their order as arbitrary and not meaningful as such.

8. Timaeos 51A.

9. See my "The Idea of Perfection in the Western World," Princeton University Press, 1946, p. 29 ff.

Chapter V

1. Aristotle discovered, however, the true nature of the potential, when he was confronted with the problem of Infinity. Here he recognized that potentiality as infinite does not ever realize itself in "actuality," but remains an infinite potentiality.

2. Aristotle, Physics: 192a18: ἐφίεσθαι καὶ ὀρέγεσθαι.

3. That the symbolic structure of truth does not exhaustively express the knowledge "about reality" was discovered by Kant who confronted the categorical synthesis of thought by an "X," given to thought and throwing its findings into the twilight of appearance, requiring the compromise of a "schema" and needing "imagination" in order to approach reality. Appearance and imagination will play their role in the following pages, although somehow different from the Kantian approach.

4. That reality itself is revealed beyond mere knowledge about it, will be seen when we have risen to the full level of a reality in which we participate. (p. 143)

5. Page 73f.

6. Page 70.
7. See furthermore p. 94.
8. On the difference between process and operation see p. 70.
9. See page 73f.
10. See also page 95 and the chapter on Creation (VIII), where the dynamism of spiritual experience, not of reflective observation, discloses a substantial process, which is neither merely sensuous nor merely intellectual and which manifests the interaction of objective and absolute forces in rhythm and melody, stable as well as in progress.
11. p. 74.
12. Statistical laws of probability have invaded even the most exact Science, Physics which prides itself on having replaced causality by a probable necessity, thus adopting the organizing principle of life. This is true. But there is a certain difference of emphasis in both cases: laws in the sciences of life are lastly concerned with the individual and his probable career, elucidated by the group and its averages, while Physics emphasizes the group-average as such and considers the individual only as absorbed in the group and constitutive for it. Physics therefore concentrates on such group-entities and imagines them when not observable, as f, i, quanta, fields, wave-packages etc., in which the individual differences are cancelled out and a probable necessity of the average has been achieved. The Sciences of life, however, use the group average only in order to interpret the direction of the individual career. Thus chance and necessity are present, although in different accentuations, in all Sciences. But it was wrong to regard this accidental or probable necessity as "freedom." Freedom is in none of these indeterminacies; neither do the electrons act freely nor does the scientist interpret freely his statistics. Knowledge "about reality" is not free. (P. 72)

13. Motion and living duration are, of course, not reversible in the sense of turning backwards. But the "momentum," indeed, radiates from the present into the past as well as into the future (p. 82).

14. The infinite outreach which Kant calls "Vernunft" and which breaks the fences of sense-experience in order to grasp an objective beyond is indeed of a very different kind than the abstract "Verstand," but it does not—as Kant thought—feign merely its objective as a "Vernunft-Idea of Totality." This objective is by no means a "totality," a "whole" which would indeed be a mere construction of our abstract intelligence (p. 21), but rises before our infinite striving as a reality, not to be labelled by abstract terms, but experienced as a guiding and ruling power.

15. Confessions XI, 33 and 39.

16. God alone was regarded as the fountain of existence, in which things merely participated. Our daily language also restrains from using "existence" with regard to things: A table does not "exist in the room," it "is" in the room, and the word "is" signifies the place in the essential abstract space-order. It is a perversion to confuse existence with spatial place. The World exists, and so does God; Man as a person exists as imbued with Divine power.

Chapter VI

1. See page 74.
2. See page 57.
3. P. 11.
4. P. 113.
5. The incarnation of the ideal of progress and future in a person should not be confused with the throwing off of this ideal and the submission to a person who is the exponent of the mad power-drive, mentioned above, and who

will be a plaything of this power-drive, himself destroyed by it in the end.

6. See p. 126.
7. See p. 104.
8. See page 88.
9. Page 71.
10. See pp. 148, 159, 202; and my "Symbol and Metaphor in Human Experience." Princeton University Press, 1949.
11. Not Ethics, Art and Religion are meaningful when ordered in analogy to scientific organization: On the contrary, the scientific organization receives justification by being analogically structured to the order of the living communion as presented in Ethics, Art and Religion.

Chapter VII

1. In a similar way the "subject" was as well the ground of the propositional process as also took a place in the proposition.
2. See Psalm 18, 23ff where God responds to the various needs of man. Cusanus emphasizes God's readiness to respond whenever needed. The concept of God's "repentance" is also of importance here.
3. See my "Symbol and Metaphor" page 93ff.
4. In the book of Job mythology transforms the hero into an innocent victim of the devil, but in the course of the story Job is elevated to a tragic, free and responsible sufferer, open to faith and the grace of God.
5. P. 83.
6. It is a confirmation of this holiness of man and of the care for man, that, according to the Gospel, Christ on the day of Judgment distinguishes between those who are blessed

and those who are damned according to the care they took of their suffering neighbor, who assumes in this suffering the stature of Christ himself. "What you have done unto the least of my brethren, you have done unto me." The loving communion with God has found its fulfillment in the devotion which man has for man.

7. Genesis 24:56; 28:20. Job 3:23; 12:24. Psalms 27:11; 37:5; 86:11; 119:24. Proverbs 2:8; 5:21. Isaiah 2:3; 42:24, etc.

8. Anselm's ontological proof starts in faith, is carried by faith and expresses rather the limits of reason and its embeddedness in an existence beyond reason, than a subjection of God and existence to reason. The latter rationalization, however, is found in St. Thomas' cosmological proofs.

9. This relative existence, as the predication of locus, is not really "existence." Kant's "dollar existing in the purse" adds indeed a predication and this predication of locus belongs to the definition of this specific dollar. Kant used this example wrongly when he attempted to disprove the ontological proof; for the absolute existence in the "proof" has nothing in common with the relative existence of locus. This absolute existence, not Kant's relative existence, surpasses proving and predication. (See also footnote 8).

10. See also p. 182.

11. See De Rougemont, "Love in the Western World."

Chapter VIII

1. See p. 138.
2. Kant's subjection of the free person to a moral law, of which the person in its turn is the law-giver, reflects the very same problem.
3. See p. 168.
4. A "good work of art" is less than a "beautiful work

of art," for we mean by it the adequacy of the work to the plan of its master; we are critical. This use of "good" with regard to a work is not the same as in the field of ethics, where it pointed to a person in a limited perspective; nor is it identical with the meaning of the "beautiful" which was the full expression of personality. Words are ambiguous.

5. See on shame and shyness page 161.

6. The integration of matter and form is in the artwork more effectively achieved than in other forms of culture as f.i. in the events of history and the deeds in the ethical realm which are shot through with non-cultural, accidental elements and therefore only point to the never fully realized meaning of history and to the never exhaustibly manifested goodness of the person. The work of art, however, creates a situation which fully realizes the cultural meaning of history and the loving value of personality, thus achieving the unique integration of matter and form, both present and both transcended.

7. See page 143.

8. See page 99.

9. See page 144f.

10. "The web of our life is of a mingled yarn, good and ill together; our virtues would be proud, if our faults whipped them not; and our crimes would despair, if they were not cherished by our virtues" (Shakespeare, "All's well that ends well," Act IV, Scene 3).

11. Shakespeare's wisdom combined, therefore, Comedy and Fairy tale in his finest works of this kind: "Midsummer Night's Dream" and "The Tempest."

12. See p. 101.

13. That the sacramental aspect is neither identical with ritual and symbol nor with the mythological contemplation which "expression" provides, was mentioned above p. 103, 150. It is therefore a mistake to regard an artwork as an

"expression" of an underlying reality. The artwork **is** this reality, it does not merely **express** it, and we share in it, involved in its sacramental devotion. It neither needs nor lends itself to the interpretation which the mythological expression elicits.

14. See my "Symbol and Metaphor in Human Experience." Not the mere blurring of qualities or conceptual differences in an undifferentiated "duration" brings the substantial energy to the fore, as Bergson's vitalism believed, but the tension of interacting and in their interaction sacrificed elements, metaphorically disclosing a new insight.

15. See p. 120.

16. If this vitalistic mood with its suspense and surprise pushes to the fore from its material setting, then the art-work sinks to a lower level. That suspense and surprise do not really belong to the essence of the work is testified by the fact that masterworks gain in every new experience of them, which would not be the case, if suspense and surprises were important. For these surely weaken in every subsequent repetition.

17. See p. 194.

18. The ornament is a mere accompaniment of something else and is as such limited. Its limitation will point to either the temporal or the spatial rhythm, and the preference of the one or the other will be dictated by the object which is to be ornamented or accompanied. So it may happen that an ornamental rhythm affects us badly when used for one object and nicely when used for another. An ornament will be especially displeasing when overdone and thus drowning its object in its part-rhythm. Such an overdoing will be most annoying when the ornament assumes the role of a self-sufficient art-work as if it were a true painting or a sculpture. In such a case the work will show a certain emptiness of abstraction, as this happens in some "non-representative

works" in which we detect only ornamental qualities and miss the full abundance of the melody.

19. Although it is the integration of spatial and temporal rhythm which is the essence of every art-work of whatever kind it may be, we can nevertheless discern a difference of attitude concerning space and time and classify accordingly: Architecture builds its sublime interior as if it rounded out a "World" for men to live in and in which to have their profoundest experiences together; and similarly myth and epic (novel) construct an all-comprehensive setting, in which generations are born, die, fight, and love. Sculpture presents a corporeal thing in its closedness, isolated, however, in order to reach beyond its enclosure into the surrounding space, and it does this through the rhythm of its contour as an expression of its lonely longing beyond; it is here that the lyrical poem conveys a similar experience, for it also expresses the longing of the creature, closed in its individual estrangement. Painting at last merges things and bodies into a ground which as a necessity of fate conveys to every object its destiny as if it were alive, sucking it into this ground from which it receives significance. Just so tragedy and drama will submerge the players into a ground of fateful necessity which in destroying them gives them dignity. Music will, like poetry play on all these registers; it will shape the wide setting of its oratorio like an epic or an architectural interior; it will express the loneliness of the creature in its songs and the drama in its symphonies.

20. Cézanne expresses excellently this unity of spatial and temporal rhythm, of color and lines: "Le dessin et la couleur ne sont plus distincts; au fur et à la mesure que l'on peint, on dessine; plus la couleur s'harmonise, plus le dessin se précise. Quand la couleur est à sa richesse, la forme est à sa plenitude." (Gasquet, "Cézanne," p. 123).

21. The size or length of an art-work is determined by the strength of inspiration, necessary to imbue it with life. But also our bodily limitations have to be taken into consideration. The spatial arts have to adapt their works to the capacity of the eye to take in and hold together. The temporal arts, like music and poetry, have to consider the limitations of attention and memory. The "heavenly length" of a Schubert movement is no artistic failing though it asks for much concentration. The genius will know when to stop, and he will detach himself the more freely from this one work, inasmuch as he is open to other works, still to be done.

INDEX

Absolute, 8, 13, 18, 20f, 31, 172
Abstraction, 4, 6f, 65
Accident, 7f
Aeschylos, 155
Aggregate, 20f
Analogy, 15, 142, 224
Analysis, 12, 49
Anselm, 232
Appearance, 75f
A priori, 39
Archimedes, v
Architecture, 235
Aristophanes, 222
Aristotle, 12, 16, 26, 29f, 32, 55, 59, 64, 66, 68, 81, 91, 95, 123, 214, 222, 225, 228
Artwork, 186f
Atom, 9

Beauty, 189f, 232f
Being, vi, 4, 15, 51
Bergson, vii, 15, 93, 95f, 234
Body, 83, 160f, 189
Brahma, Brahmin, vii, 75, 98, 150

Calvinism, 114
Cantor, 21, 23
Care, 159, 190
Causality, 36, 225
Cezanne, 235
Chance, 75

Character, 131, 185
Choice, 113
Church, 155
Class-concept, 224
Coherence- and Correspondence- theory, 227
Comedy, 198
Communication, 213
Communion, 128, 178, 192, 204
Concept, 45f
Concrete, 79, 149
Conscience, 165
Consciousness, 68f, 74
Construction, 25
Contingency, 101
Continuity, 24, 89
Conversion, 154
Creation, 101f, 177f
Cult, 155
Culture, 139
Cusanus, 231

Death, 114f, 163, 175
Decision, 124
Deduction, 50
Demiurgos, 12
Democritos, 9
Demoniac, 153
Density, 24
Descartes, 23, 34, 108, 218, 222
Desire, 105

Difference, 13f, 47f, 226
Dike, 8, 16, 112
Dimension, 23, 32
Discovery, 176
Dogma, 156
Dostoevsky, 156
Doubt, 64
Drama, 197
Dream, 109
Duration, 80
Duty, 165

Effect, 36
Emotion, 93
Empiricists, v, 22
Entelechy, 59, 123
Entropy, 98
Epic, 197
Equality, equation, 20, 37, 45
Eros, 64
Error, 106
Eternity, 101, 207
Ethics, 162f
Evil, 153f
Exclusion, 10
Existence, Existentialists, 15, 99, 134, 187, 230
Expression, 102, 233f
Expressionism, 197
Extension, 27f, 30

Fact, 3ff
Fairy-tales, 199
Faith, 119, 133f, 216
Fate, 102
Fichte, 116
Force, 58, 120, 205
Form, 56, 177f, 194
Francis, St, 151
Freedom, 72, 106, 111f, 122, 145
Function, 20f
Future, 55, 88, 94

Genius 212
Geometry, 25

God, 16, 39, 150, 180f
Good, 6, 171, 182
Grace, 152
Guilt, 165

Harmony, 209
Hegel, 107, 127
Heidegger, 99, 114
Heracleitos, 16, 222
Here-now, 30f
History, 117f
Hobbes, 45
Humor, 199
Hypothesis, 51

Idea, 6
Identity, 11, 13, 49, 223
Imagination, Images, 76f
Impressionism, 197
Indivisibility, 29
Induction, 50
Infinite, 20f
Inherent accidents, 35
Intensity, 80, 82f
Intention, 43, 167
Intercession, 148, 155, 193
Intuition, vii, 27, 79, 226
Invention, 176
Irreversibility, 93

Kant, v, 11, 21, 30, 55, 107, 123, 143, 184, 222, 228, 230, 232
Knower and known, 68f, 141f

Law and Instances, 49f, 170
Leibniz, v, 11, 95, 116
Life, 68f
Logic, 13, 19, 49
Love, 105, 129, 162, 173f, 180
Lyrical, 197

Magic, 103
Magnitude, 32
Many, 18f
Mathematics, 19f

Matter, 14, 56, 138, 177, 194
Meaning, 44f
Measurement, 32
Melody, 203f
Memory, 82, 88
Metaphor, 148, 202
Method, 20
Michelangelo, 195
Momentum, 82f, 230
Mood, 90
Mortality, 150
Motion, 24, 81f, 97
Mozart, 198, 207
Mythology, 16, 30, 89, 102f

Nature, 78, 95, 189
Necessity, 16, 19, 36
Negation, 107
Negative Theology, vii
Newton, 22
Nietzsche, 122, 153
Nirvana, vi
Nought, vi, 8, 22f, 99
Numbers, 20f

Objectivity, v, 12
One, 18f
Operation, 20, 23, 70
Order, 12, 14f, 16
Ornament, 234
Orphism, 8, 222

Painting, 235
Pantheism, 64
Parmenides, 4, 11, 12, 108
Part, 21, 37
Particular, vi, 47
Pascal, 23
Passion, 105
Past, 55, 88, 94
Paul, St., 154
Perception, 78
Perfection, 22, 57, 170
Permanence, 55
Personality, 130, 172, 188, 205

Physics, 85, 229
Plato, v, vii, 6, 9, 12, 14, 23, 32, 36, 64, 66, 95, 105, 108, 125, 180, 182, 216, 224
Play, 5, 193
Possession, 173, 220
Possibility, 16, 19, 36, 224
Potentiality, 26, 66
Power, 58, 126
Predestination, 114
Predicate, 48
Present, 55, 88
Privation, 68
Probability, 85f
Problem, 64
Process, 10, 16, 19, 46, 70, 187
Progress, 119
Proposition, 43f
Psychology, 6, 22, 109
Purpose, 54, 181
Pythagoras, 20, 24, 222, 225

Question, 64

Reality, 67
Regress, 23, 38, 225
Relation, **10f, 130**
Rembrandt, 195, 210
Repentance, 166, 231
Representation, 148
Responsibility, 119
Revelation, 149
Rhythm, 91, 203f
Risk, 169
Ritual, 103, 150f

Sacrifice, 150, 158, 169, 175
Sacrament, 150, 160, 202
Sartre, 109, 114
Science 9, 13, 58f
Sculpture, 235
Sensation, 77
Service, 144, 168, 175, 213
Shakespeare, 214, 233
Shame, 161, 191

Shyness, 161, 191
Sign, signification, 14
Sin, 152f
Situation, 124
Sophocles, 155
Space, 10, 25, 28
Spinoza, 33, 95, 162
Stoics, 39, 108, 111f, 227
Structure, 11
Style, 194f
Subject, 48, 231
Sublime, 198
Substance, 34
Sum, 19f
Syllogism, 224
Symbol, 52, 101, 148, 200f, 228
Synthesis, 12, 49
System, 39

Tao, 150
Tempo, 90

Thing, 83
Thomas, St., 224
Thought, 6f, 12, 43
Time, 24, 28
Totality, 21, 39, 230
Tragedy, 16, 112, 154, 198
True, Truth, 6, 44, 118, 189
Tyche, 8, 16

Unconscious, 73f
Uniqueness, 133, 179
Universal, vi, 46f, 224

Vacuum, 9
Value, 178
Verification, 49, 227

Whitehead, 95
Whole, 21, 37, 56
Will, 106, 171
Works, 181f
World, 97f

Washington School of Psychiatry, Inc.